Buonissimo!

Tasty and Easy Italian Food for Every Occasion

Gino D'Acampo

photography by Kate Whitaker

kyle books

To Luciano and Rocco:
The best things I've ever made.

This edition published in 2009 by
Kyle Books, an imprint of Kyle
Cathie Ltd
1818 Newkirk Avenue, Suite 1G ,
Brooklyn, New York 11226
www.kylecathie.com

Distributed by National Book
Network, 4501 Forbes Blvd.,
Suite 200, Lanham,
MD 20706
1.800.462.6420

10 9 8 7 6 5 4 3 2 1
978-1-904920-89-2

Text © 2008 Gino D'Acampo
Photography © 2008 Kate Whitaker
Book design © 2008 Kyle Cathie Limited

Editorial Director Muna Reyal
Designer Carl Hodson
Photographer Kate Whitaker
Food stylist Nicole Herft
Props Liz Belton
Copy editor Stephanie Evans
Production Director Sha Huxtable
The Library of Congress Cataloging-in-Publication Data is available on file.
Color reproduction by Chromagraphic
Printed and bound in China by C&C Offset.

Introduction 6

Romantico
Elegant recipes for two 11

Per me
Recipes for one 43

Per tutti i giorni
Everyday suppers 74

Facile facile
Easy but impressive recipes 107

Salute
Party food for sharing 138

Conversion chart 172
Index 173
Acknowledgments 175

Introduction

I cannot believe that it has been a year since I wrote my first book, *Fantastico!* and here I am again writing the introduction to my second one. The first thing I want to do is thank all of you who supported me. *Fantastico!* received the Gourmand Cookbook Award for the Best Italian Cookery Book in the World in 2007, but even more inspiring has been the response to my recipes in that book. I hope you like this one just as much!

So why is this book called *Buonissimo*? Well, it means something that is very tasty, and of course in this case, we are talking about food, and Italian food in particular.

Over the last year, I have spent a lot of time in Italy with students and other chefs, trying to get as much inspiration as possible, and creating easy and tasty recipes for every occasion. Some of the recipes have come from my grandfather's old notes that he left me and I am very proud that I can share them with all of you.

I have tried to write recipes not just from Naples, the town I come from, but also from the other regions of Italy. I have taken traditional recipes and, using my philosophy of keeping things simple and not using too many ingredients, made them my own.

For this book, I also wanted to make sure there are recipes for every occasion. I believe food should play a huge part in our lives, as a celebration, to bring comfort and to seduce, as well as nourish and sustain us. So there are five chapters in this book, which I hope will suit every kind of person, for every type of meal.

If you want to impress somebody, then the recipes in *Romantico* are for you. These are recipes for two people, full of luxurious ingredients, and much more effective than a bunch of flowers. And I think these recipes will also work even if the meal isn't romantic, but a special meal for your mother, best friend, or boss.

Per Me are recipes for one person, whether you live alone or when everyone else has gone out and you want a simple, tasty meal just for yourself. Often you can make a big batch and save the rest for another time. On the other hand, *Salute* is the party chapter. Here are finger food recipes for lots of people or elegant appetizers for a dinner party.

Facile Facile and *Per Tutti I Giorni* are just the opposite. These are chapters for quick and easy recipes that use pantry ingredients and provide ideas for comforting family suppers for weekdays. If you make sure you have a good choice of these ingredients on hand, you should be able to make any of these recipes on short notice.

The last thing I want to do is remind you that there is no such thing as a bad cook. You just need to believe in yourself, choose the right ingredients, and, of course, use this book! Cooking impressively does not have to be difficult—I promise you, you won't get stressed in my kitchen, but your guests will love you!

And my rules for success: pour yourself a nice glass of wine, throw everyone else out of the kitchen, make sure your ingredients are fresh and of good quality and that your knife is sharp and, finally, only cook if you are in a good mood.

In this book, you will find recipes that are *Buonissimo* and once you have tried them, you will understand my motto:

Minimum effort, maximum satisfaction!

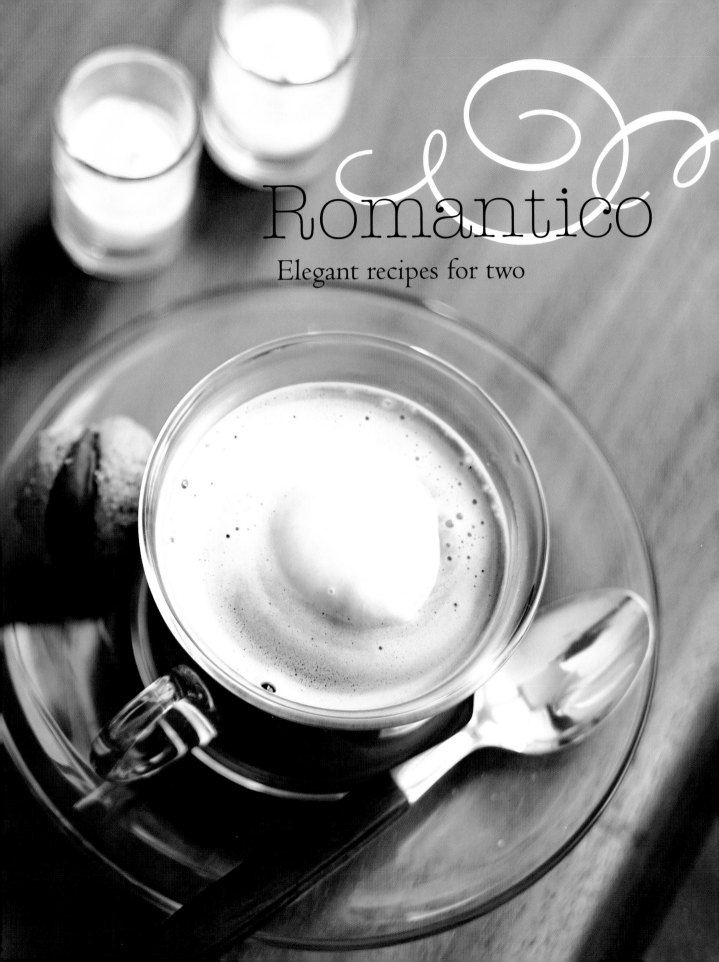

Romantico

Elegant recipes for two

This was, of course, the easiest chapter for me

to write, as Italians are born with natural romantic style. I wrote this for all of you who need that little bit of help to show your loved one what they mean to you or for those of you who are trying to catch the girl or boy of your dreams. Apart from choosing the right recipe, getting the wine right is an essential part of a romantic dinner. Make sure you dress for the occasion, set the scene with the right music, and don't forget the most important rule—you are there to spoil your partner. Good luck, and if things don't go quite as planned, don't blame the food!

Topolini al Tartufo e Salvia

SERVES
2

If you really want to show your partner that you have made lots of effort to prepare a romantic dinner, this is the dish to make. It takes a little more time than the others, as you literally prepare it from scratch, but it's so worth it. If you really don't like truffles, leave out the truffle-flavored olive oil, but please make sure the Parmesan cheese is freshly grated and not the dried packaged stuff you can buy in tubs. Great for vegetarians.

Little Gnocchi with Truffle Oil, Butter, and Sage

Topolini al Tartufo e Salvia SERVES 2

10½ ounces russet potatoes, unpeeled

1 small egg, lightly beaten

¾ cup all-purpose flour, plus extra for dusting

7 tablespoons salted butter

4 ounces mixed wild mushrooms

1 tablespoon finely sliced fresh sage leaves

2 tablespoons truffle-flavored olive oil

¼ cup freshly grated Parmesan cheese

Salt and freshly ground black pepper

Put the potatoes in a large saucepan, cover with cold water, and bring to a boil. Cook for 25 to 30 minutes, until tender. Drain well and leave to cool slightly.

Peel the potatoes and press through a potato ricer into a large bowl. While the potatoes are still warm, add 2 pinches of salt, the egg, and flour. Lightly mix, then turn out onto a floured surface. Knead lightly until you have soft, slightly sticky dough. (Do not overwork it or the little gnocchi will be tough.)

Cut the dough in half and roll each piece into a long sausage shape, about ½ inch in diameter. Slice into ¾-inch pieces.

Lay the topolini on a lightly floured clean dish towel.

Bring a large saucepan of salted water to a boil. Drop in the topolini, a few at a time, and cook for about 2 minutes. They are ready as soon as they float to the surface.

Meanwhile, melt the butter in a large frying pan over medium heat. Once hot, stir in the mushrooms and cook for 2 minutes before adding the sage. Season with salt and pepper and remove the pan from the heat.

Add the topolini to the frying pan and toss well.

Divide between two serving plates, drizzle with the truffle oil, and serve sprinkled with the Parmesan. Great with a glass of Prosecco.

Spicy Carrot Soup with Garlic Croutons

Zuppa di Carote Piccante con Crostini all'Aglio SERVES 2

4 tablespoons olive oil

½ onion, chopped

9 ounces carrots, peeled and cut into ¼-inch cubes

1 teaspoon chili powder

1½ cups vegetable stock

2 garlic cloves, crushed

2 slices of white bread, crusts removed and cut into ½-inch cubes

Salt

Heat half the oil in a saucepan and gently sauté the onion for 3 minutes, stirring occasionally. Add the carrots with the chili powder and continue to cook for an additional 5 minutes, stirring occasionally.

Pour in the stock, bring to a boil, and gently cook, with the lid on, for about 45 minutes.

Meanwhile, heat the remaining oil in a frying pan, add the garlic, and cook over a low heat for 30 seconds. Add the bread cubes, turn the heat to medium, and toss together for a few minutes until golden brown all over. Toss frequently. Drain on paper towels, and keep warm.

Purée the soup in a food processor until smooth and season with salt. Return the soup to the rinsed-out saucepan and reheat gently.

Serve hot, sprinkled with the garlic croutons.

Fresh and Tasty Tomato Salad

Insalata di Pomodori e Origano SERVES 2

4 large, beautifully ripe plum tomatoes

¼ cup good-quality extra virgin olive oil

1 teaspoon dried oregano

Coarse sea salt and freshly ground black pepper

Use a sharp knife to slice the tomatoes into ¼-inch rounds and arrange on a serving plate. Drizzle over the oil, season with salt and pepper, and sprinkle with the oregano.

Leave to marinate, at room temperature, for at least 20 minutes before dishing up. Serve with crusty bread to mop up all the juice.

I know many people who don't really like the taste of shellfish but are always very impressed with this recipe because, with the black pepper coating, the scallops become less fishy than usual. The fresh Italian salsa is a combination that you will never forget and is a perfect main course for a romantic dinner. To get the best flavor, make sure you use good pitted black olives and do not overcook the scallops, otherwise they will lose their tenderness.

Scallops Coated in Black Pepper with Salsa

Capesante al Pepe con Salsetta SERVES 2

FOR THE SALSA

2 tablespoons olive oil

1 garlic clove, thinly sliced

2 large plum tomatoes, chopped, seeds and skin included

1 ounce black olives, pitted and cut in half

1 tablespoon salted capers, rinsed

5 basil leaves, sliced

Salt

FOR THE SCALLOPS

6 tablespoons fine breadcrumbs, toasted

⅛ cup all-purpose flour

3 tablespoons black peppercorns, crushed

2 medium eggs, beaten and seasoned

8 scallops (ask your fishmonger to clean them)

4 tablespoons olive oil

2 tablespoons salted butter

Extra virgin olive oil for drizzling

To make the salsa, heat the olive oil in a medium frying pan and cook the garlic over medium heat until golden. Add the tomatoes, olives, and capers, season with salt, and cook for about 3 minutes. Stir in the basil and remove the salsa from the heat. Set aside to cool.

Meanwhile, mix the breadcrumbs, flour, and black pepper together on a plate and have the eggs ready in a bowl.

Wash the scallops under cold running water and pat dry on paper towels. Dip each one first into the egg, then coat in the breadcrumb mixture.

Heat the oil with the butter in a large frying pan and fry the scallops over high heat for about 1 minute on each side. Once they look brown and crunchy, transfer to paper towels to drain any excess oil.

To serve, place the salsa in the center of two serving plates and arrange 4 crisp scallops on top. Drizzle with extra virgin olive oil and accompany with warm crusty bread.

I absolutely love tempura recipes and I think that oysters made tempura-style are amazing. Of course, let's not forget that this dish will be a great romantic starter because oysters are an aphrodisiac. You can prepare the batter a good hour ahead, but please cook your oysters just before serving.

Oysters in Sesame Seeds and Black Pepper Tempura

Ostriche Fritte con Salsetta al Soya SERVES 2

10 Pacific oysters

3½ cups sunflower oil for deep-frying

¼ cup all-purpose flour

¼ cup cornstarch

1 tablespoon crushed black peppercorns

2 tablespoons sesame seeds

About ½ cup ice-cold sparkling water (from a new bottle)

1 lemon, cut into 6 wedges

Salt

FOR THE DIPPING SAUCE

3 tablespoons dark soy sauce

3 tablespoons cold water

Juice of 2 lemon wedges (see above)

To open the oysters, cover your hand with a dish towel, hold the shell, and insert the tip of a sharp knife into the muscle between the two halves. Remove the oyster and place on paper towels to dry. (Keep the deeper shells for serving.)

Make the dipping sauce by mixing the soy sauce, water, and the juice from 2 of the lemon wedges in a small bowl and divide between 2 dipping saucers.

Heat the oil in a medium, heavy-bottom saucepan to about 375°F (if you don't have a cooking thermometer, the oil is hot enough when a piece of bread dropped into the oil turns brown in 30 seconds).

Meanwhile, sift the flour and cornstarch into a large bowl with a pinch of salt. Mix in the black pepper with the sesame seeds and start to pour in the cold sparkling water. Stir everything together until just mixed and still a little lumpy. (Make sure the batter is very thin—it should be almost transparent around the oysters.)

Dip the oysters, one at a time, into the batter and fry in the hot oil for no longer than 1 minute. Drain on paper towels and place in the reserved shells.

Serve immediately with the dipping sauce and remaining lemon wedges, accompanied by your favorite green salad.

If you think that any romantic dish should involve using your fingers, this is definitely the ultimate finger-licking recipe. The only thing you will have to be careful about is to cook this on the day you buy the shellfish so that they are really fresh—and never on a Monday because it won't be fresh from the market. You can use fresh tomatoes instead of canned and, of course, you can substitute fresh chiles for the dried chiles.

Quick Stew of Mussels and Clams

Impepata di Cozze e Arselle SERVES 2

2 tablespoons extra virgin olive oil, plus extra for brushing

3 garlic cloves (2 thinly sliced, 1 left whole)

½ teaspoon crushed dried chiles

14 ounces canned chopped tomatoes

⅛ cup cold water

10 ounces mussels, cleaned (discard broken ones and any that do not close when tapped firmly)

10 ounces clams, cleaned (discard broken ones and any that do not close when tapped firmly)

2 tablespoons dry white wine

2 tablespoons chopped fresh flat-leaf parsley

2 slices white rustic bread (preferably ciabatta)

Salt to taste

Heat the oil in a large saucepan over medium heat and cook the sliced garlic and chiles for about 20 seconds. Add in the chopped tomatoes with the water and leave to simmer, uncovered, for 8 minutes.

Meanwhile, place the mussels and clams in a second large saucepan on the heat and pour in the wine. Cover with a lid and cook for 5 minutes, until the shellfish have opened.

Once ready, transfer the shellfish into the pan with the tomato sauce. Include the cooking juices but do not pour in the last few spoonfuls of the juices in case there is any grit. Stir well together, add the parsley, and leave to rest for 1 minute.

Brush the sliced bread with a little olive oil, place on a hot grill pan, and toast on both sides until crisp and smoky. Once ready, rub the slices with the whole clove of garlic and place in two soup bowls. Spoon the shellfish and sauce on top of the bread and serve immediately with your favorite glass of cold white wine.

I know that many people worry about cooking a dish that involves any kind of pastry, but please trust me when I say that this is the easiest recipe to prepare and your partner or friend will not be disappointed with the presentation and, of course, the flavor. The biggest tips I can give you are to make sure that your salmon is very fresh and that your oven has been preheated.

Salmon and Creamy Leek Pastries

Fagottini di Salmone e Porri SERVES 2

2 leeks, trimmed and chopped

4 tablespoons salted butter, plus extra for brushing

3½ ounces mascarpone cheese

6 sheets filo pastry (8 x 8 inches)

2 tablespoons unsalted butter, melted

2 skinless salmon fillets, about 3oz each

Salt and freshly ground black pepper

Cook the leeks in a large frying pan with 3 tablespoons of water and the butter for about 10 minutes. Season with salt and pepper and stir occasionally. Transfer from the pan to a bowl and leave to cool.

Preheat the oven to 400°F.

Once the leeks have cooled, mix in the mascarpone cheese.

To assemble the pastries, brush a sheet of filo with melted butter, then lay 2 more sheets on top, brushing with butter between each layer. Place a salmon fillet in the center, season with salt and pepper, then spoon half the leek mixture on top of each fillet. Fold the pastry ends over the top, pull up the sides, and scrunch together to enclose the filling. Brush both pastries with melted butter.

Place the pastries on a lightly greased baking sheet and bake in the middle of the oven for 20 minutes, until browned and crisp.

Serve with your favorite green salad.

It is very traditional, especially in northern Italy, around Pisa, to cook asparagus in puff pastry. I got this recipe about twenty years ago when, for the first time, I went to visit the famous tower of Pisa. It was a family friend who prepared it for us, and I remember he told me that he won his wife with this dish. How romantic! Only use fresh asparagus for this dish, and you can substitute the Parmesan for Pecorino if you prefer.

Asparagus and Ricotta Tarts

Tartine di Asparagi e Ricotta SERVES 2

1 sheet frozen puff pastry, defrosted

5½ ounces ricotta cheese

¼ cup freshly grated Parmesan cheese

6 sun-dried tomatoes in oil, drained and finely chopped

10 asparagus spears

2 tablespoons extra virgin olive oil

1 tablespoon chopped fresh chives

Salt and freshly ground black pepper

Preheat the oven to 400°F.

Unroll the pastry and cut in half. Roll each half out to a 6 x 4-inch rectangle. Use a knife to mark out a smaller rectangle on each piece, big enough to hold 5 asparagus spears. (Do not cut through the pastry.) Use a small sharp knife to mark the borders in a neat lattice pattern. Transfer to a baking sheet.

Bake the pastry in the middle of the oven for about 15 minutes until just puffy and slightly colored. Remove, set aside to cool slightly, then gently depress the risen pastry with the back of a fork.

Lightly mix together the ricotta with the Parmesan. Gently fold in the sun-dried tomatoes and season with salt and pepper.

Trim the asparagus spears to fit the pastry. Divide the ricotta mixture between the two pastry cases. Place the asparagus spears on top and slightly press into the ricotta mix.

Drizzle with the extra virgin olive oil and bake for 20 minutes.

Sprinkle the tarts with the chives and serve hot or at room temperature accompanied by a salad.

SERVES
2

Honey Chicken Liver Salad with Sherry Vinegar

Insalata di Fegatielli e Pinoli SERVES 2

2 tablespoons olive oil

10½ ounces chicken livers

2 ounces pine nuts

3½ ounces arugula leaves

1 tablespoon sherry vinegar

1 tablespoon honey

Salt and freshly ground black pepper

Heat the olive oil in a large frying pan and start to cook the livers with the pine nuts over medium heat for about 6 minutes. Season with salt and pepper and stir occasionally to help the liver cook evenly.

Meanwhile, divide the arugula leaves between two serving plates.

Once the chicken livers are cooked, turn off the heat and pour in the sherry vinegar with the honey. Use a wooden spoon to deglaze the pan by stirring everything about and scraping the bottom of the pan.

Serve the livers on top of the arugula leaves and pour over the juices from the pan.

Perfetto with a big glass of red wine.

Honey-glazed Carrots with Macadamia Nuts

Carote Smielate SERVES 2

2 large carrots, peeled and cut into ½-inch rounds

5½ ounces shallots, peeled

1 tablespoon salted butter

10 macadamia nuts, halved

1 tablespoon honey

Salt and freshly ground black pepper

Bring a medium saucepan of salted water to a boil and cook the carrots and shallots for 3 minutes. Drain.

Melt the butter in a large frying pan and add the shallots, carrots, and nuts. Season with salt and pepper, and cook over a medium heat for 5 minutes, stirring occasionally.

Pour in the honey and continue to cook, over a higher heat, for an additional 2 minutes.

Serve hot with your favorite main course or cool to room temperature and mix with salad greens.

If you need a tasty and impressive recipe with not a lot of washing up to do, this is the one to try. Fish always goes down well for a fabulous romantic dinner because it's light and tasty and cooks quickly. Make sure you have a good bottle of cold Italian wine to accompany it.

Roasted Monkfish with Baby Leeks and Cherry Tomatoes

Coda di Rospo e Porri al Forno con Pomodorini SERVES 2

8 baby leeks, trimmed and washed

2 x 7-ounce monkfish fillets (off the bone), scaled and skin on

2 tablespoons fresh rosemary leaves, stripped from the stalks

2 tablespoons fresh thyme leaves

3 tablespoons extra virgin olive oil

1 small lemon, quartered

10 cherry tomatoes

Salt and freshly ground black pepper

Bring a saucepan of salted water to a boil and cook the leeks for about 3 minutes. Drain in a colander and allow to steam dry.

Place the fish in a large bowl with the herbs, olive oil, and lemon quarters and season with salt and pepper. Add in the leeks, toss well, and leave to rest for 15 minutes.

Meanwhile, preheat the oven to 400°F. Put in a roasting pan to warm up.

Place the fish, skin-side down, on the preheated roasting pan and pour over the rest of the ingredients from the bowl. Roast for 15 minutes, then remove the fish and keep warm.

Add the cherry tomatoes to the roasting pan and continue to roast the leeks for an additional 5 minutes.

Remove the pan from the oven and pile the leeks onto two warm serving plates. Place the fish on top and drizzle with the cooking juices.

Arrange the cherry tomatoes around the plates. Serve immediately with a cold glass of Pinot Grigio.

This recipe is for Nicole, who gave me the inspiration for it. Scallops are one of the most romantic ingredients you can cook—luxurious, soft, and succulent. They have a very delicate taste, so you don't want too many strong flavors with them, but the salty pancetta will go with it perfectly. You can leave the roe in if you don't want to waste anything.

Creamy Scallops with Pancetta

Capesante alla Nicoletta SERVES 2

3½ tablespoons butter

1 onion, diced

¼ cup heavy cream

Vegetable oil for frying

1 large leek, trimmed and cut into thin matchsticks

3½ ounces diced pancetta

6 large scallops, cleaned, roe removed

Salt and freshly ground black pepper

Melt half the butter in a frying pan. When it foams, add the onion and cook over low heat for 15 minutes, until the onion is soft but not colored. Stir in the cream and cook for 2 more minutes. Blend to a smooth purée and keep warm.

Heat the vegetable oil in another frying pan and pan-fry the leek until slightly colored and crisp. Remove from the pan and drain on paper towels. Fry off the pancetta for 2 to 3 minutes or until it begins to crisp up. Remove from the pan and pour out any excess fat.

Season the scallops. Return the frying pan to the heat, and add the remaining butter to the hot pan along with the scallops. Fry the scallops for 10 to 15 seconds on one side, or until they start to caramelize. Flip the scallops, add the pancetta, and remove from the heat.

Place 2 tablespoons of the onion purée in the center of each warmed plate. Arrange 3 scallops on the purée and spoon over the pancetta along with some of the buttery juices. Top with a small handful of the crisp leeks.

Serve immediately with a cold glass of champagne!!

This is one of my mother's special Sunday recipes. I remember when I was a child, my father would go to the fish market to buy the fresh shrimp, bring them home, and I would wait impatiently for my mum to cook them in this delicious sauce. This is what I call a romantic dish.

Jumbo Shrimp in Caper and Tomato Sauce

Gamberoni alla Marinara SERVES 2

3 tablespoons olive oil

3 canned anchovy fillets in oil, drained

1 garlic clove, thinly sliced

2 tablespoons pitted Kalamata black olives

1 tablespoon salted capers, rinsed and drained

14 ounces canned chopped tomatoes

1 teaspoon dried oregano

8 large jumbo shrimp (head and shells on)

Salt and freshly ground black pepper

Heat the oil in a large frying pan and cook the anchovies until they dissolve. Add the garlic and continue to cook until soft and golden. Stir in the olives and capers. Pour in the chopped tomatoes with the oregano, season with salt and pepper, and simmer, uncovered, for about 15 minutes. Stir occasionally.

Add the shrimp to the sauce and continue to cook gently for 4 minutes. Turn the shrimp over and cook for another 4 minutes.

Place some of the sauce in the middle of two serving plates and top with 4 shrimp. Try to cross 2 shrimp together so that they sit up on the plate.

Accompany the dish with your favorite salad and some warm crusty bread, and enjoy with a glass of cold Prosecco.

The first time I cooked this recipe was about five years ago, and even today I still believe that this is my lucky dish. It was the recipe that I cooked on my first-ever television show and it is still a big hit with the ladies. I know you may ask how a plate of pasta can be a big hit with the ladies and my answer is very simple, trust me—I'm Italian! You can substitute ground beef or lamb for the pork and you can stuff the pasta a good couple of hours in advance.

Stuffed Pasta Shells

Conchiglioni Ripieni SERVES 2

5½ ounces dry conchiglioni (10 shells)

½ onion, finely chopped

3 tablespoons olive oil

9 ounces ground pork (or beef or lamb, if you prefer)

9 ounces béchamel sauce (you can use store-bought)

14 ounces canned chopped tomatoes

8 basil leaves

½ cup freshly grated Parmesan cheese

Salt and freshly ground black pepper

Boil the pasta in boiling salted water for about 5 minutes. Drain, place on a clean dish towel, and leave to cool.

Sauté the onion in a large frying pan in 2 tablespoons of the olive oil until golden brown. Add the ground pork and mix well, allowing the meat to crumble. Cook, stirring frequently, for 15 minutes, until the meat has browned. Remove from the heat and leave to cool.

Once the meat has cooled down, pour half of the cold béchamel sauce into the pan and mix with the meat.

Put the tomatoes in a small saucepan and heat through. When bubbling, add the remaining olive oil, and the basil and season with salt and pepper. Cook for no longer than 3 minutes.

Preheat the oven to 350°F.

Pour the tomato sauce into the bottom of an ovenproof dish (this prevents the pasta shells from sticking).

Use a tablespoon to fill the conchiglioni with the meat mixture and gently place them in the dish. Make sure the shells aren't too close together. When you have filled the dish, drizzle the pasta with the remaining béchamel and cover the dish with foil.

Bake for about 20 minutes. Remove the foil, sprinkle with the Parmesan, and cook for an additional 5 to 10 minutes, or until the cheese is golden.

Serve immediately by spooning some of the tomato sauce into the center of a serving plate and arranging the pasta shells on top.

What can I say about this recipe? Everyone has tried it, most people love it, but not many people know how to cook it properly. If you read the ingredients list, you have probably realized that there is no cream in this recipe—that's how you cook a traditional spaghetti carbonara. For romantic effect, serve all the pasta in a large bowl, sit close, and share.

Pasta with Smoked Pancetta, Eggs, and Pecorino Romano

Spaghetti alla Carbonara SERVES 2

1 tablespoon extra virgin olive oil

3½ tablespoons salted butter

3½ ounces smoked pancetta, rind removed, cut into small pieces

9 ounces dry spaghetti

3 large egg yolks, beaten

2 tablespoons finely chopped fresh flat-leaf parsley

¼ cup freshly grated Pecorino Romano cheese

Salt and freshly ground black pepper

Heat the oil and the butter together in a large frying pan over medium heat. Add the pancetta with a pinch of black pepper and fry until very crisp, stirring occasionally.

Meanwhile, cook the pasta in a large saucepan with plenty of boiling salted water (for up to 10 ounces pasta allow at least 3½ quarts water) until al dente. Once the pasta is cooked, drain thoroughly and place in the hot frying pan with the pancetta.

Remove the pan from the heat, pour in the eggs with the parsley, and keep stirring until you create a creamy texture. Season lightly with salt (go easy because the pancetta can be quite salty). Serve immediately, topped with the grated cheese.

There are two things that my wife can't get enough of. First, well I leave it to your imagination. Second is this dish. Traditionally this recipe is cooked with white wine, but one day I didn't have any and the only bottle I had in the fridge was sweet Martini Bianco—what a wonderful experiment. Try veal instead of chicken, and if you don't have sweet vermouth, you can use a good Marsala wine. Make sure that the chicken is thin, so it cooks fast and doesn't get tough.

Chicken Breast in Martini Sauce

Scaloppine di Pollo al Martini SERVES 2

2 medium skinless chicken breasts

¼ cup all-purpose flour

4 tablespoons salted butter, plus a little extra for the sauce

½ cup Martini Bianco (sweet)

Salt and freshly ground black pepper

Place the chicken breasts on a cutting board, cut in half horizontally, and lay a piece of plastic wrap on top. Use a meat mallet to flatten the breasts to a thickness of ¼ inch.

Put the flour on a flat plate and season with salt and pepper.

Melt the butter in a large frying pan over medium heat.

Lay the chicken breasts in the seasoned flour and lightly coat on both sides. Place in the pan and gently fry in the butter for about 3 minutes on one side. Turn over and cook for an additional minute.

Pour in the Martini and using a long kitchen match, flame the alcohol. Allow the alcohol to burn off, then cook for an additional 2 minutes and season with salt.

Place the scaloppine on a serving plate.

Add an extra pat of butter to the pan. Mix well over medium heat then pour immediately over the chicken.

I like to serve this with a simple salad of spinach leaves dressed with extra virgin olive oil, a squeeze of fresh lemon juice, and a pinch of sea salt.

Whenever I need to be forgiven by my wife, I know that there are only two things that can save me—an expensive present or my beef tenderloin with flamed brandy. She absolutely adores it and I also think she likes to see a man flaming in her kitchen. Well, I'm going to dedicate this recipe to all the men out there that need to be forgiven and hope it works for you. Please, please do not overcook the tenderloins, otherwise the recipe will be completely ruined.

Beef Tenderloin with Flamed Brandy and Green Peppercorns

Filetto al Pepe Verde e Brandy con Patate al Forno SERVES 2

FOR THE OVEN FRIES

2 baking potatoes, scrubbed and cut into thick shapes

2 sprigs of fresh rosemary

3 garlic cloves, unpeeled and slightly crushed

2 tablespoons olive oil

Salt and freshly ground black pepper

FOR THE TENDERLOIN

2 teaspoons coarsely ground black pepper

2 beef tenderloins, about 5½ ounces each

1 tablespoon olive oil

4 tablespoons butter

2 tablespoons brandy

2 tablespoons dry white wine

¼ cup beef stock

1 tablespoon green peppercorns in brine, drained

5½ tablespoons heavy cream

Preheat the oven to 450°F.

Place the potatoes, rosemary, and garlic on a large non stick baking sheet. Drizzle over the olive oil, season with salt and pepper, and cook in the middle of the oven for 30 minutes, until the fries are cooked through and crisp. Check and turn them occasionally.

Meanwhile, rub the coarsely ground black pepper all over the tenderloins.

Heat the oil with 2 tablespoons of the butter in a medium frying pan. As soon as the butter stops foaming, add the steaks. Cook for 4 minutes on each side for a medium steak, or for 3 minutes if you like it rare. Transfer the steaks to a warm plate, season with salt, and set aside in a warm place to rest for 3 minutes.

Pour the excess fat from the pan then add the brandy. Using a long kitchen match, flame the alcohol. Allow the alcohol to burn off, then stir the pan, scraping the meat juices off the bottom of the pan. Pour in the white wine and reduce by half.

Add the stock and continue to cook over high heat, stirring occasionally, until the sauce is well reduced.

Stir in the peppercorns, cream, and remaining butter. Cook for an additional 2 minutes, stirring continuously.

Pile the potatoes in the middle of two serving plates and top each one with a tenderloin. Pour over the sauce and serve immediately with a glass of dry red wine.

Come on, this is the romantic chapter, so of course I had to put in a banana recipe, and I couldn't think of anything better than crisp chunks of banana served with a delicious caramel sauce. Unfortunately, you will not be able to cook the bananas ahead, so you need to prepare them at the last minute but they do say, good things come to those who wait, and whoever is waiting for this won't be disappointed. If you like, you can use apples instead.

Banana Fritters with Quick Caramel Sauce

Frittelle di Banana SERVES 2

FOR THE CARAMEL SAUCE

6½ tablespoons salted butter

1 cup brown sugar

½ cup heavy cream

FOR THE FRITTERS

1 cup self-rising flour

1 egg, beaten

¾ cup cold sparkling water (don't open the bottle until the last minute)

2 bananas, cut into 1¼-inch chunks

Oil for deep-frying

Confectioners' sugar for dusting

To make the sauce, place the butter, sugar, and cream in a small saucepan. Bring to a boil, then reduce the heat and simmer for 3 minutes. Set aside.

Sift the flour into a bowl, make a well in the center, and add the egg and the sparkling water all at once. Stir until all the liquid is incorporated and the batter is free of lumps.

Heat the oil in a deep heavy-bottom pan. When a cube of bread browns in 15 seconds it is hot enough.

Dip the bananas in the batter a few pieces at a time, drain off any excess, and gently lower the pieces into the hot oil using a slotted spoon. Cook for about 2 minutes, or until golden, crisp, and warmed through.

Carefully remove the fritters from the oil with the slotted spoon and drain on paper towels. Repeat with the remaining banana pieces.

Serve the fritters immediately with the caramel sauce and dusted all over with plenty of confectioners' sugar. Fantastic with a little glass of Vin Santo or any other dessert wine.

I can still see myself as a teenager sitting outside a bar in my home town of Torre del Greco, having this exquisite dessert with all my friends from school. This is the one to choose if you want to impress someone with something easy to make. Make sure you use a good-quality vanilla ice cream, and if you don't like Amaretto liqueur, try Baileys instead.

Vanilla Ice Cream with Hot Espresso, Amaretto, and Grated Chocolate

Affogato al Caffe e Amaretto SERVES 2

1 pint good-quality
vanilla ice cream

2 shots freshly made
espresso

2 tablespoons
Amaretto liqueur

2 teaspoons grated
good-quality dark
chocolate

Drop 2 scoops of ice cream into two stemmed glasses or cappuccino cups. Pour over the freshly made hot coffee and 1 tablespoon of the Amaretto liqueur per serving.

Sprinkle the affogato with grated chocolate and serve immediately with chocolate cantuccini or your favorite Italian cookies.

PS: Affogato has to be made with proper strong espresso coffee, so unless you have the right machine, save the pleasure for the next time you are at my house or in an Italian restaurant.

I must have been about sixteen, and I can remember it like it was yesterday—my first exam at my catering school. The night before I could not sleep, thinking about what I was going to prepare for my exam and, knowing that the judge was a lady, I thought a hot chocolate fondant should do the job. Well... I was right—I came first in the class and got about six dates with girls who wanted to try it!

Hot Chocolate Fondants Stuffed with Chocolate Truffles

Paradiso di Cioccolato SERVES 2

3½ ounces good-quality dark chocolate (70 percent cocoa solids)

3½ tablespoons salted butter, at room temperature

3 tablespoons ground almonds

2 tablespoons cornstarch

1 egg, separated

3 tablespoons superfine sugar

1 tablespoon Amaretto liqueur

3 good-quality chocolate truffles

Confectioners' sugar, for dusting

Preheat the oven to 325°F.

Finely grate about 1 ounce of the chocolate onto a plate.

Rub half of the butter all over the inside of 2 tall dariole molds, dust well with the grated chocolate, shake any excess, and set aside on a baking sheet.

Melt the remaining chocolate plus any leftover grated chocolate and the remaining butter in a large heatproof bowl set over a pan of simmering water.

Remove the bowl from the heat and beat the ground almonds, cornstarch, and egg yolks into the melted chocolate.

In a separate large, clean, dry bowl, beat the egg white until soft peaks form. Gradually whisk in the superfine sugar.

Fold the meringue mixture and the Amaretto liqueur into the melted chocolate mixture.

Gently spoon half of the mixture into the molds, place a chocolate truffle on top, then continue to fill the molds, leaving a gap of about ¼ inch at the top.

Bake the fondants in the middle of the oven for 20 minutes, until risen and slightly wobbly.

Turn the fondants out onto 2 serving plates, dust liberally with confectioners' sugar, and serve hot.

Per Me

Recipes for one

Coming home from the studios one evening

after recording *Ready Steady Cook*, a taxi driver recognized me and we started talking about food. One of the things he said really frustrated him was that no one seemed to write books for people who live on their own or for that one night when you only need to cook for one. He explained that following a recipe that was created for four but using smaller amounts of ingredients never seemed to work. I couldn't agree more with him so here they are... recipes for the nights you are alone but still want to cook something nice. I have also created recipes that you can make in big batches and freeze very easily so you can defrost and heat up anytime you want during the week. So for those who live on their own—there is no longer any excuse not to get in the kitchen and start cooking.

After a great boys' night out, this is probably the best dish to have, either when you come back or when you finally get up in the morning. Of course it reminds me of my playboy days, long, long ago. The unique combination of Brie with the crispy pancetta is absolutely *Buonissimo*, though you can definitely substitute bacon for the pancetta, or a sharp cheddar cheese for the Brie. Try to serve my eggs as shown in the photograph.

Playboy Eggs

Uova alla Playboy SERVES I

4 slices pancetta, 2 chopped into small pieces

1 tablespoon olive oil, plus extra for greasing

2 ounces button mushrooms, quartered

1 scallion, sliced on the diagonal

1 ounce ripe Brie cheese, cut into small chunks

2 fresh eggs

Salt and freshly ground black pepper

Preheat the oven to 400°F and grease a cappuccino cup with a little olive oil.

Place the two whole slices of pancetta on a baking sheet and bake in the oven until golden and crispy. Leave to cool until firm.

Heat the olive oil in a medium frying pan and cook the mushrooms and chopped pancetta for about 5 minutes, until golden. Add the scallion, season, and cook for an additional 3 minutes, stirring continuously. Remove from the heat and stir in half the cheese.

Pour the mixture into the greased cup, then break the eggs in the cup, keeping the yolks whole. Place on a baking sheet and bake, uncovered, for 5 minutes.

Remove from the oven, sprinkle the remaining cheese over the eggs, and bake, uncovered, for an additional 8 minutes.

Once ready, stand the slices of crispy pancetta on either side of the cup so that they look like the ears of the playboy bunny. Sprinkle with black pepper.

Serve immediately with your favorite bread.

Apart from quickly boiling the beans, there is not really a lot of cooking for this recipe, so you have no excuses for not getting these few ingredients together and making this wonderful salad. I often assemble this dish when I can't really be bothered to cook and I'm in need of something fresh, colorful, and tasty. If you prefer, you can substitute chunks of mozzarella for the goat cheese and you can also add any nuts that you like.

Green Bean Salad with Mint, Goat Cheese, and Pine Nuts

Fagiolini alla Menta con Formaggio di Capra e Pinoli SERVES I

3½ ounces green beans, trimmed

½ garlic clove

3 fresh mint leaves

2 tablespoons extra virgin olive oil

1 tablespoon freshly squeezed lemon juice

3 ounces firm goat cheese

2 tablespoons pine nuts, toasted in a dry frying pan

Salt and freshly ground black pepper

Cook the beans in boiling salted water until al dente.

Meanwhile, finely chop the garlic and the mint together and place in a large bowl. Pour in the oil and lemon juice and mix together until well combined.

Drain the beans well and add to the bowl with the dressing. Season with salt and pepper and toss everything together until evenly coated.

Transfer the salad to a serving plate, crumble over the goat cheese, and scatter with the cooled pine nuts. Enjoy with some warm crusty bread.

Herbed Potato Pancakes with Bubbling Goat Cheese

Crocchette di Patate e Formaggio di Capra SERVES I

7 ounces russet or Yukon Gold potatoes, peeled

2 teaspoons chopped fresh thyme leaves, plus 1 or 2 sprigs for garnish

1 scallion, finely chopped

2 tablespoons olive oil

2 tablespoons salted butter

2½ ounces firm goat cheese

Salt and freshly ground black pepper

Coarsely grate the potatoes, then use your hands to squeeze out as much of the thick starchy liquid as possible. Place into a large bowl and combine with the thyme and chopped scallion. Season with salt and pepper.

Divide the mixture into two and shape into two flattish discs about ¾ inch thick.

Heat the oil and the butter in a frying pan. Lower the potato pancakes into the pan, spacing them well apart, and cook over medium heat. Press firmly down with a spatula and cook for 4 minutes on each side until golden.

Preheat a grill pan over medium heat.

Once the pancakes are ready, cut the cheese in half horizontally and place one half, cut side up, on each potato cake. Grill for about 3 minutes, until lightly golden.

Transfer immediately to a serving plate, garnish with thyme sprigs, and accompany with some arugula leaves.

Warm Potato and Crispy Bacon Salad

Patate e Pancetta MAKES 4 PORTIONS, BUT WILL KEEP WELL IN THE FRIDGE FOR A FEW DAYS

3½ ounces baby new potatoes, scrubbed

1 tablespoon olive oil

5 strips bacon

½ tablespoon grainy mustard

1 tablespoon white wine vinegar

1 scallion, thinly sliced

¼ cup pumpkin seeds

Salt and freshly ground black pepper

Bring a large saucepan of salted water to a boil and cook the potatoes for about 18 minutes, or until tender. Drain and cut in half.

Meanwhile, heat the oil in a frying pan and cook the bacon until very crisp. Transfer to a plate and allow to cool. Cut into small pieces.

Place the warm potatoes in a large bowl and pour in the mustard and vinegar. Add in the scallion and half of the bacon. Season with salt and pepper and toss everything together.

When you are ready to serve, transfer the salad to a large serving dish. Sprinkle with the pumpkin seeds and the remaining crisp bacon.

When I first came to London, I could not understand why anyone would mix a boiled shrimp with mayonnaise and the other ingredients that go into a shrimp cocktail sauce. Now I am completely converted, but of course I could not stick to the original recipe—I had to put my Italian twist to this classic British dish. Make sure you use big juicy shrimp and good-quality green pitted olives.

Italian Shrimp Cocktail

SERVES 1

1 tablespoon mayonnaise

1 tablespoon heavy cream

½ teaspoon tomato paste

1 teaspoon freshly squeezed lemon juice

Dash of Worcestershire sauce

1 teaspoon small capers in brine, drained

1 tablespoon green pitted olives, chopped

8 cooked peeled shrimp

Handful of lettuce leaves, shredded

Slices of lemon, to garnish

Salt and freshly ground black pepper

Put the mayonnaise into a bowl and mix in the cream, tomato paste, lemon juice, Worcestershire sauce, capers, and olives.

Fold in the shrimp and season with salt and pepper.

At the last minute, fold in the lettuce and transfer immediately to a large Martini glass garnished with lemon slices.

Buonissimo with slices of toasted brown bread.

The worst thing you can do to asparagus is to overcook it, unless of course, you're making this wonderful soup. Never, ever try to create this dish with canned asparagus because you will completely lose the freshness of the dish. I chose this soup for this chapter first of all because of the taste, and second because if there is any left over, you can freeze it as long as you use it up within ten days.

Spring Chilled Asparagus Soup

Zuppa di Asparagi SERVES 1, FREEZE THE REMAINING SOUP

14 ounces asparagus

2 tablespoons salted butter

2 onions, chopped

3½ cups vegetable stock

7 tablespoons heavy cream

Zest of 1 lemon, to garnish

Salt and white pepper

Cut the tips from the asparagus stalks, about 2 inches from the top. Drop into a medium saucepan of boiling salted water and cook for 3 minutes. Drain and immediately refresh in cold water. Set aside.

With the help of a potato peeler, scrape the asparagus stalks and discard the woody ends. Chop the remaining stalks.

Melt the butter in a large saucepan and cook the onions with the chopped stalks over medium heat for 10 minutes. Stir occasionally.

Pour in the stock and season with salt and pepper. Bring to a boil and simmer over medium heat for 35 minutes, or until everything is tender. Once cooked, allow to cool.

Pour the soup into a blender or food processor and puree until smooth. Pass through a sieve into a bowl and then stir in the cream.

Cover the bowl with plastic wrap and refrigerate for 2 hours.

Garnish with the reserved asparagus tips and a few strands of lemon zest and serve. Any remaining soup can be frozen.

I love liver, but the problem I have with it is that most of the time people try to do too much with it, or even worse, they overcook it. This is a very traditional Italian way to cook liver and, in my family, it is the only way we cook it. Please, please, please do not use dried sage because it will completely ruin this dish.

Calf Liver with Black Pepper, Butter, and Sage

Fegato al Burro, Salvia e Pepe SERVES 1

8 cherry tomatoes on the vine

3 tablespoons olive oil

1 slice ciabatta

3 tablespoons all-purpose flour, for dusting

3½ ounces calf liver

2 tablespoons salted butter

4 fresh sage leaves

Handful of mixed salad leaves

Salt and freshly ground black pepper

Preheat the oven to 400°F.

Place the cherry tomatoes on a small roasting pan. Drizzle with 1 tablespoon of the olive oil, season well, and place in the oven for 5 to 10 minutes, until soft and slightly roasted.

Next, grill or toast the ciabatta and set aside.

Place the flour on a plate and use to coat the liver on both sides.

Heat the remaining olive oil in a medium frying pan over high heat. Once hot, cook the liver for 30 seconds on each side or, if you like your liver well done, cook for 50 seconds on each side.

Lower the heat to medium, wipe out any oil left in the frying pan, and add the butter and sage leaves. Season with salt and plenty of black pepper. Continue to cook for about 40 seconds, just until the butter is completely melted.

Dress the liver with the butter and sage sauce and serve immediately on top of the ciabatta, so that the bread can soak up the lovely buttery juices. Perfect with your favorite salad and the roasted cherry tomatoes.

SERVES
I

I think that as I get older I like curries more and more. I have to admit that I can only manage a medium-hot one, but slowly, slowly I'll get there. When I first came to England, I didn't really appreciate the fantastic flavors of spices and, now, fourteen years later, I've written this recipe, which I've very proudly named Italian Bean Curry. You can use dried beans, but I think the canned ones work perfectly for this kind of dish.

Italian Bean Curry

Fagioli al Curry SERVES 1. FREEZE THE REMAINING 3 PORTIONS

2 tablespoons olive oil

¼ cup good-quality curry paste

1 x 14-ounce can coconut milk

7 tablespoons vegetable stock

7 ounces (drained weight) canned cannellini beans

7 ounces (drained weight) canned borlotti beans

7 ounces (drained weight) canned lentils

3 scallions, thinly sliced

2 large plum tomatoes, skinned and cut into ½-inch cubes

Lime wedges, to garnish

Put the oil in a medium saucepan over medium heat and add the curry paste. Cook for 3 minutes, stirring occasionally.

Pour in the coconut milk with the stock, bring to a boil, and simmer, uncovered, for 5 minutes. Add in the beans, lentils, onions, and tomatoes. Continue to simmer for an additional 5 minutes, stirring occasionally.

Serve with plain rice of your choice, with a lime wedge on top.

Most of my food memories growing up in Italy consist of seafood. We ate it almost every day because we lived by the coast—I always remember this particular dish because I used to go fishing with my uncle (Mazza Tosta) who used to be (and I hope still is) the master of cooking razor clams. The combination of garlic, chile flakes, parsley, and clams works beautifully, especially if you serve it with a good country-style bread.

Razor Clams with Olive Oil, Lime, and Chile

Cannollicchi alla Zio Salvatore SERVES 1

2 slices country-style bread

3 tablespoons olive oil

Pinch of dried chile flakes

8 razor clams, washed but still in their shells

1 tablespoon finely chopped fresh flat-leaf parsley

1 garlic clove

Lime wedges, to garnish

Sea salt

First toast the bread on both sides in a toaster or under the broiler. Leave to cool slightly.

Heat the oil with the chile flakes in a large frying pan and add the clams in a single layer, hinge side down.

Once the clams have completely opened, turn them over, making sure the meat comes into contact with the base of the pan. Sprinkle with the parsley and a little sea salt and cook for 1 minute, or until the clams are lightly browned.

Meanwhile, rub the garlic clove over one side of the toasted bread.

Serve the clams immediately with the garlic toasted bread and the fresh lime wedges, and enjoy with a cold glass of Italian beer.

I have to admit that I don't often cook sea bream. I usually order it when I'm out in a restaurant, especially when I'm in the south of Italy, but ever since I put this recipe together, I cook it at least twice a month. I love the way the rosemary and the garlic work with the fish and, even better, it cooks in only twenty minutes. You can substitute sea bass for the sea bream, and make sure you drizzle it with a good-quality extra virgin olive oil.

Roasted Sea Bream with Rosemary and Garlic

Orata al Forno con Aglio e Rosmarino SERVES 1

1 whole sea bream (about 1 pound), scaled and gutted

5 sprigs fresh rosemary

2 garlic cloves, unpeeled and halved

2 tablespoons olive oil

2 ounces arugula leaves

¼ fennel bulb, thinly sliced

¼ radicchio, roughly chopped

1 lemon, half for juicing, half for serving

1 tablespoon extra virgin olive oil

Coarse sea salt and freshly ground black pepper

Preheat the oven to 400°F.

Place the fish on a cutting board and use a sharp knife to slash each side twice diagonally.

Insert 3 of the rosemary sprigs and all the garlic into the cavity and stick the remaining rosemary into the slashes. (Allow these seasonings to hang out of the fish so that they too will roast, giving extra flavor to the dish.)

Place the fish in a roasting pan, drizzle with the olive oil, and sprinkle with sea salt. Roast in the oven for 20 minutes, or until the flesh is white and the skin is crisp.

Meanwhile, dress the arugula leaves, fennel, and radicchio in a bowl with the juice of half the lemon and the extra virgin olive oil. Season with salt and pepper and mix well.

Serve the fish hot from the oven accompanied by a beautiful fresh salad and the other half of the lemon.

I know that it may sound a bit cheesy to dedicate a recipe to yourself, but really, guys, this is the kind of dish that I like to prepare when I'm on my own and I'm in need of something tasty and easy. Make sure you rest the steak for a good minute after it has been cooked, allowing the meat to get tender, and dress and season the aragula leaves just before you are ready to eat.

Sliced Steak with Cherry Tomatoes, Arugula, and Balsamic Vinegar Dressing

Tagliata alla Gino SERVES 1

1 sirloin steak
(about 9 ounces)

3 tablespoons extra
virgin olive oil

5 cherry tomatoes,
washed and halved

2 ounces arugula
leaves

1 tablespoon good-
quality balsamic
vinegar

10 pieces freshly
shaved Parmesan
cheese

Salt and freshly
ground black pepper

Rub the steak with 1 tablespoon of the oil and make little cuts along the fat to prevent the meat from shrinking and curving as it cooks.

Preheat a grill pan until hot and cook the steak for 2 minutes on each side for medium (add an extra 2 minutes on each side if you prefer your steak well done). Season with salt and pepper and place the steak on a cutting board to rest for 1 minute.

Meanwhile, place the tomatoes and arugula leaves in a large bowl, pour over the remaining oil, season with salt and pepper, and mix well with your fingertips. Arrange the salad on a serving plate.

Use a sharp knife to cut the steak into ¾-inch slices and lay on the salad. Drizzle over the balsamic vinegar and scatter with the Parmesan.

Serve immediately with a cold beer.

SERVES
I

I wanted to write this recipe mainly because I want people to know that brussels sprouts should not just be eaten because they are good for you. They can be used all year round and, combined with the right ingredients, are a delicious side dish to any main course, especially a meat one. You can try this recipe with carrots or fresh fennel instead of Brussels sprouts.

Brussels Sprouts with Garlic ✓ Breadcrumbs and Pecorino

Cavoletti Gratinati SERVES 1

4 ounces Brussels sprouts

3 tablespoons extra virgin olive oil, plus extra for drizzling

3 tablespoons dried breadcrumbs

3 tablespoons freshly grated Pecorino Romano cheese

2 tablespoons finely chopped fresh flat-leaf parsley

1 garlic clove, finely chopped

Salt and freshly ground black pepper

Preheat the oven to 425°F.

Cook the Brussels sprouts in boiling salted water for 5 minutes. Drain thoroughly.

Drizzle 2 tablespoons of the oil in an ovenproof oval dish just big enough to hold all the sprouts.

Mix together the breadcrumbs, cheese, parsley, garlic, and the remaining oil in a small bowl. Season with salt and pepper. Sprinkle the mixture over the Brussels sprouts.

Put the dish in the middle of the oven and cook for 15 minutes.

Remove from the oven, drizzle with a little more oil, and serve as a main dish or to accompany a meat dish of your choice.

..r you come in late from work and you are starving, this is a really quick and filling meal to prepare, yet it doesn't sit heavily on your stomach because of the freshness of the lemon and the lightness of the zucchini. Make sure that once the pasta is combined into the sauce, you serve it immediately, otherwise it will get soggy. I have also tried this recipe without the Parmesan cheese and it works fine. And, of course, make sure the spaghetti is al dente.

Zucchini and Lemon Zest Pasta

Spaghetti con Zucchine e Buccia di Limone SERVES I

1 zucchini, coarsely grated

3 tablespoons olive oil

Good pinch of dried chile flakes

2 tablespoons pine nuts

Zest of ¼ lemon

4 ounces spaghetti

2 tablespoons freshly grated Parmesan cheese

Salt

Put the grated zucchini in a clean dish-towel and squeeze dry.

Heat the oil in a large frying pan and cook the zucchini for 5 minutes over medium heat, stirring occasionally. Add the chile flakes, pine nuts, and lemon zest and continue to cook for an additional 3 minutes. Season with salt and stir.

Meanwhile, cook the pasta in a large saucepan with plenty of boiling salted water until al dente. Once the pasta is cooked, drain thoroughly and add to the frying pan with the zucchini.

Toss everything together over medium heat for 30 seconds. Serve immediately, sprinkled with Parmesan.

If you feel like making yourself a really special meal, this is the one for you. The prosciutto will keep the chicken breast from drying out in the oven, and as you are by yourself, you won't have to worry about garlic breath! If you love this recipe, you can easily double or quadruple the quantities and make it for your friends and family.

Chicken Wrapped in Prosciutto with a Creamy Herb Sauce

Pollo Avvolto con Prosciutto Crudo SERVES 1

1 bulb garlic

2 tablespoons olive oil

3 slices prosciutto

1 skinless, boneless chicken breast

¾ cup hot chicken stock

7 tablespoons heavy cream

1 tablespoon chopped fresh flat-leaf parsley

1 tablespoon chopped fresh basil

Handful of green beans, steamed, to serve

Salt and freshly ground black pepper

Preheat the oven to 350°F. Place the entire bulb of garlic in a square foil with 1 tablespoon of the olive oil. Wrap it up securely and place in the oven for about 30 minutes, or until the bulb has softened completely and can be pulled apart and the garlic from each clove can be squeezed out.

Lay the prosciutto slices beside each other, slightly overlapping. Season the chicken breast with salt and pepper and place it in the middle of the ham. Fold the slices over the chicken so that it is evenly wrapped.

Heat the remaining olive oil in a frying pan and cook the chicken for 2 to 3 minutes on each side. Transfer to an ovenproof dish and bake in the oven for an additional 15 minutes. Remove from the oven and allow to rest.

In a small pan, reduce the chicken stock by half, and add the cream and 3 cloves of roasted garlic. (Keep the rest of the garlic and mix with mayonnaise for a quick garlic mayo.) Reduce by half again and strain. Stir through the chopped herbs.

Serve the steamed beans on a warmed plate, place the chicken on top, and spoon the sauce over. Enjoy!

I've dedicated this dish to a fantastic woman called Tina Silvagni, who is my best friend's mother. She always says how much she likes to cook anything with lamb, especially lamb cutlets. Personally, this is my favorite cut of lamb. Make sure you marinate the meat for at least thirty minutes and do not overcook the cutlets, otherwise they will be quite tough. If you want, you can use the same marinade for pork chops.

Lamb Cutlets Tina-style

Abbacchietti alla Tina SERVES I

5 lamb rib chops

2 tablespoons olive oil

2 pinches dried chile flakes

2 tablespoons pitted Kalamata olives, sliced

1 garlic clove, sliced

2 pinches dried oregano

Zest and juice of ½ small lemon

Salt and freshly ground black pepper

Use a meat mallet to gently flatten the chops and place them in a large non-metallic bowl. Pour in the oil, add the chile flakes, olives, garlic, oregano, and lemon zest and juice. Season with salt and turn the chops in the marinade to coat both sides. Leave to marinate at room temperature for 30 minutes.

Once ready, scrape the marinade from the chops, reserving the marinade. Heat a frying pan and cook the chops for 2 minutes on each side, until they are beautifully colored.

Pour the reserved marinade with 2 tablespoons water into the pan and continue to cook the chops over medium heat for 2 minutes on each side. (This timing will give you medium-rare meat.)

Place the chops on a warm serving plate and pour over the juices from the pan. Serve immediately with a tasty potato salad (see page 51) and a cold beer.

This is what I call the ultimate comfort food. I bet anyone who doesn't like chicken livers that they will absolutely love this dish, and you can eat it at any time of the day. The secret is to make sure that you serve it with good-quality breadsticks (see page 142) or warm crusty bread.

Garlic Chicken Liver Paté with Green Peppercorns

Pate di Fegatini di Pollo all'Aglio e Pepe SERVES 1, FREEZE THE REMAINING 5 PORTIONS

3½ tablespoons salted butter

1 pound chicken livers, trimmed

½ teaspoon dried oregano

4 garlic cloves, crushed

2 tablespoons brandy

1 tablespoon freshly squeezed lemon juice

1 tablespoon green peppercorns in brine, drained and finely chopped

Salt

Melt the butter in a large frying pan and add the livers, oregano, and garlic. Cook over medium heat for 10 minutes, stirring occasionally.

Pour in the brandy and set alight with a long kitchen match. Allow to flame for 5 seconds. Once the flame is out, remove from the heat and stir in the lemon juice. Allow to cool slightly.

Transfer the contents of the pan into a blender or a food processor and puree until smooth. Season with salt.

Stir the chopped peppercorns into the paté.

Spoon equally into 6 ramekins, cover with plastic wrap and refrigerate for 2 hours.

Buonissimo with homemade cheesy breadsticks (see page 142).

Freeze the remaining pâté in the ramekins for up to 10 days.

I often prepare this dish when I'm on my own, simply because it cooks very quickly. I don't need too many ingredients and the taste is unbelievable. I know that gammon steak (from the hindleg of the pig) is quite an old-fashioned cut, but trust me, it will not disappoint, and like everything in life the old-fashioned way is normally the best. You can substitute a pork chop or chicken breast for the gammon steak and if you don't like mascarpone, just use any other soft cheese.

Spicy Gammon Steak with Mascarpone Peas

Bistecca di Pancetta al Peperoncino con Crema di Piselli SERVES 1

2 tablespoons olive oil

2 teaspoons salted butter

¼ teaspoon dried chile flakes

1 tablespoon finely chopped fresh flat-leaf parsley

1 gammon steak (about 6 ounces)

½ cup frozen peas, defrosted

2 tablespoons mascarpone cheese

Salt and freshly ground black pepper

Heat half the oil and half the butter in a medium frying pan. Add the chile flakes and half the parsley. Cook the gammon steak for 3 minutes on each side. Transfer to a warm serving plate and pour over the juices from the pan.

Wipe out the pan with some paper towels, and return to the heat with the remaining oil and butter. Add the peas and cook over high heat for 2 minutes, tossing continuously.

Season with salt and pepper, and add the mascarpone cheese and remaining parsley. Turn off the heat and use a fork to roughly mash the peas into the mascarpone.

Place the mushy peas next to the gammon steak and serve.

Creamy Rice Pudding with Amaretto and Toasted Almonds

Risotto Dolce all'Amaretto e Mandorle SERVES 1

1¾ cups skim milk

1 tablespoon superfine sugar

1½ ounces Arborio risotto rice

1 teaspoon orange zest

¼ teaspoon vanilla extract

1 tablespoon Amaretto liqueur

2 tablespoons skinned almonds

1 teaspoon brown sugar

Pour the milk and the sugar in a medium saucepan and stir over low heat until the sugar has dissolved.

Add the rice and orange zest and stir briefly. Bring to a boil, then immediately reduce the heat to as low as possible. Cook for 45 minutes, stirring occasionally. Once it looks thick and creamy and the rice is tender, stir in the vanilla extract and Amaretto liqueur. Set aside to rest for 3 minutes.

Preheat the broiler.

Meanwhile, dry-roast the almonds in a small frying pan for 2 minutes over medium heat. Shake the pan occasionally. Finely chop the toasted almonds.

Spoon the rice mixture into a heatproof cup, then sprinkle over the toasted almonds and the brown sugar.

Broil briefly until the sugar has almost melted. Serve immediately.

Strawberry, Banana, and Tarragon Smoothie

Frullato di Fragole e Banana SERVES 1

3½ ounces fresh strawberries

1 banana

Leaves from 2 fresh tarragon sprigs

5 tablespoons vanilla yogurt

handful of ice cubes

Fresh mint leaves, to decorate

Put everything, except the mint, in a food processor and blitz until creamy and smooth.

Serve in a tall glass decorated with mint leaves.

If you are looking for a dessert that you are not going to feel really guilty about eating, this is the one to choose. I know that it may sound like a lot of effort to make a meringue, but believe you me, it really is one of the easiest things to prepare. You can substitute pears for the peaches and, if peaches are out of season, just use canned peach halves.

Marzipan-stuffed Peach with Meringue

Pesca Alaska SERVES 1

1 ripe peach, halved and pit removed

⅞ ounce marzipan

1 large egg white

¼ cup superfine sugar

1 tablespoon brown sugar

Preheat the oven to 400°F.

Remove the skin from the peach by placing it cut side down on a plate. Put the plate in the sink and pour first boiling water then cold water over it. Drain immediately and peel.

Roll the marzipan into a ball and place in the hollow left by the peach pit, then press the halves back together.

In a large, clean bowl, beat the egg white until stiff peaks form, gradually add in the superfine sugar, and continue to beat until thick and glossy.

Cover the peach completely with a layer of meringue, making sure there are no gaps. Use a fork to rough up the surface of the meringue.

Place the peach in a shallow ovenproof dish, sprinkle with the brown sugar, and bake in the middle of the oven for 18 minutes, until the meringue is lightly browned.

Serve immediately with your favorite ice cream.

Per Tutti I Giorni

Everyday suppers

I could really have written a whole book on

everyday food, as it's very much my style of cooking. I don't believe in using fussy cooking methods and strange ingredients. All the recipes in this chapter have been tested for anyone who wants a great meal with amazing flavors any time of the day, any time of the week. There are some of my favorite pasta dishes, which will make your life simple if you need a good meal using straightforward pantry ingredients. The recipe that I'm most proud of, however, is my Italian Toad in the Hole, and in my opinion, it's the best one I've ever tried! It's easy, impressive, and massively tasty.

As I was brought up in the south of Italy, I have lived on the traditional tomato and basil bruschette, so I decided to try to create other toppings to make this appetizer or brunch dish even more exciting. I often use this recipe when I have people around for dinner, and so far it has never failed to impress. If you are not a big fan of anchovies, you can always use canned sardines, and please make sure you use a good extra virgin olive oil.

Bruschette with Roasted Pepper and Cannellini Puree, Black Olive Relish & Arugula

Bruschette SERVES 6 AS AN APPETIZER

8 tablespoons extra virgin olive oil

1 small onion, chopped

1 teaspoon smoked paprika

14 ounces canned cannellini beans, drained

2 roasted peppers (from a jar)

2 ounces pitted Kalamata olives, chopped

3 tablespoons chopped fresh flat-leaf parsley

1 tablespoon freshly squeezed lemon juice

1½ ounces arugula leaves

1 baguette, cut into ¾-inch-thick slices

Salt and pepper to taste

Heat 2 tablespoons of the olive oil in a medium saucepan and cook the onions for 5 minutes, stirring occasionally. Add the smoked paprika and cook for 2 more minutes.

Place the onion mixture, beans, roasted peppers, and 2 more tablespoons of the olive oil in a food processor and blend until smooth. Season with salt and pepper and allow to cool slightly.

To make the black olive relish, place the olives and parsley in a bowl. Pour over the remaining oil and 1 tablespoon lemon juice. Season and stir well.

Place the bread slices on a hot grill pan and cook for 2 minutes on each side, until lightly charred.

To serve, spread some of the cannellini and roasted pepper puree over each warm bruschetta and spoon on a little of the olive relish. Top with a few arugula leaves, drizzle with a touch more extra virgin olive oil, and place on a large serving plate. Perfect with a cold glass of good Prosecco.

...years of my life I didn't really eat soups, except for the odd ...vice a year, but since I've lived in England I have become a convert. ...r warming soup, which, served with some fresh warm crusty bread, goes down as one of my favorites. This is one of those dishes that, eaten the day after, is even better than the day you made it.

Chunky Winter Vegetable and Bean Soup

Zuppa di Verdure e Fagioli SERVES 4

6 tablespoons extra virgin olive oil, plus extra for drizzling

1 onion, roughly chopped

2 carrots, peeled and cut into ¾-inch chunks

2 turnips, cut into chunks

2 celery stalks, roughly chopped

5 ounces curly savoy cabbage, roughly chopped

1 bay leaf

5 cups vegetable stock

14 ounces canned cannellini beans, drained

5 ounces (prepared weight) winter squash, cut into ¾-inch cubes

¼ cup roughly chopped fresh flat-leaf parsley

4 slices of rustic country bread

1 garlic clove, cut in half

1 cup freshly grated Parmesan cheese

Salt and freshly ground black pepper

Heat the olive oil in a large saucepan and cook the onion, carrots, turnips, celery, cabbage, and bay leaf until they start to turn golden, stirring occasionally.

Pour in the vegetable stock and gently simmer for 30 minutes or until all the vegetables are soft. Stir occasionally.

Add the beans and the squash, and season with salt and pepper. Continue to cook for 15 minutes. Once ready, stir in the parsley and allow to rest for 3 minutes.

Meanwhile, place the bread on a hot grill pan and cook for about 2 minutes on each side, until golden and crisp. Immediately rub with the cut garlic clove and drizzle with some extra virgin olive oil.

To serve, place a slice of bread in each serving bowl and pour over the soup. Sprinkle with Parmesan and serve immediately.

The beautiful thing about this recipe is that you can use it for all different occasions—appetizer, breakfast, lunch, main course—anything goes. If you want to, you can substitute rainbow trout for the salmon, and please don't bother making your own fresh mayonnaise because in this recipe the ready-made one works perfectly. My only serving tip for this dish is to serve the mousse with some warm crusty bread—amazing!

Fresh Salmon and Lemon Mousse

Mousse di Salmone Fresco SERVES 8

¾ pound piece fresh salmon (tail end)

1 small onion, sliced

1 carrot, sliced

2 bay leaves

6 tablespoons dry white wine

⅔ cup cold water

3½ teaspoons granulated gelatin

1¼ cups milk

2 tablespoons salted butter

4 teaspoons all-purpose flour

5 tablespoons mayonnaise

Zest of 1 large lemon

⅔ cup heavy cream

Salt and white pepper

Place the salmon in a medium saucepan with half the sliced onion and half the carrot, 1 bay leaf, the white wine, and ½ cup of the water. Season with a little salt, bring to a boil, and gently simmer for 12 minutes.

Transfer the salmon to a plate (reserving the poaching liquid). Remove and discard the skin using a fork. Flake the fish and place in a bowl.

Boil the reserved liquid until reduced by half, then strain and reserve.

Place the gelatin sheets in a bowl and drizzle over the remaining cold water. Leave to soak for 3 minutes.

Pour the milk into a saucepan and add the remaining onion, carrot, and bay leaf. Bring to a boil and set aside to infuse for at least 10 minutes. Strain and leave to cool.

Melt the butter in a medium saucepan and stir in the flour. Cook for 1 minute, then gradually whisk in the milk. Bring to a boil and cook for about 10 minutes, whisking continuously, until it thickens. Pour into a bowl and stir in the soaked gelatin. Leave to cool.

Once ready, pour the white sauce into a blender or food processor with the flaked salmon and the reserved cooking juices. Process for just a few seconds—you want the salmon to retain a little of its texture.

Transfer the salmon mixture into a large bowl and fold in the mayonnaise and lemon zest.

Whip the cream in a clean bowl until soft peaks form and then fold into the salmon mixture.

Spoon the mousse into a soufflé dish or a bowl, cover with plastic wrap and refrigerate for 3 hours, until set.

Leave the mousse at room temperature for 30 minutes before serving. Scoop out the mousse, like ice cream, on serving plates accompanied by some warm crusty bread.

It really annoys me that couscous is not used as often as you would use rice or potato because I think it's a great ingredient that cooked in the right way, creates a wonderful dish. I learned how to make this recipe about five years ago when I was in Sicily, and this is my favorite way to use couscous. The peppery flavor of the arugula with the freshness of the lemon is an explosive combination—but always, always, always use freshly squeezed lemon juice.

Arugula and Lemon Couscous

Couscous con Rucola e Limone SERVES 6

½ cup olive oil

7 tablespoons freshly squeezed lemon juice

18 ounces couscous

8 scallions, chopped

1 cucumber, seeded and roughly chopped

5 ounces arugula leaves, roughly chopped

Zest of 1 lemon

Salt and freshly ground black pepper

Whisk together the oil and lemon juice in a small bowl, season with salt and pepper, and set aside.

Place the couscous in a large bowl and cover with 2¼ cups cold water. Drain and return the couscous into the same bowl. Leave for 10 minutes to allow the grains to swell. Once ready, fluff the grains with a fork to remove any lumps.

Place the couscous in a cheesecloth-lined metal colander and steam over a pan of boiling water for 20 minutes. Separate the grains with the fork occasionally to prevent them from clumping.

Transfer the couscous to a warmed serving bowl. Stir in the scallions, cucumber, and arugula leaves. Pour over the lemon dressing, stir well, and sprinkle over the lemon zest.

Serve immediately to accompany a meat or fish dish of your choice.

SERVES
4

I'm going to dedicate this recipe to a great friend of mine who also happens to be a fantastic teacher, Professor Graeme Turner. I remember he once invited me to dinner and he promised me that he was going to cook the ultimate Italian risotto. I have to admit that his risotto was good, but he did manage to burn himself and use at least four pans to make something that should be done in one pot. So here you have it, mate—hope it makes your risotto life easier!

Risotto with Prosciutto and Vin Santo

Risotto al Vin Santo SERVES 4

5 tablespoons olive oil

1 red onion, finely chopped

2 celery stalks, finely chopped

1 quart chicken stock (made from a stock cube if you wish)

10 ounces Arborio rice

12 ounces Vin Santo (Italian dessert wine, or a good Italian medium white wine)

2 tablespoons chopped fresh flat-leaf parsley

5½ tablespoons salted butter

1 cup freshly grated Parmesan cheese, plus extra shavings for garnish

8 slices prosciutto

Salt and freshly ground black pepper

Heat the olive oil in a large saucepan and gently cook the onion for about 5 minutes. Add the celery and cook for an additional 5 minutes until softened, stirring occasionally.

Meanwhile, bring the stock to a simmer and adjust the seasonings. Keep hot.

Add the rice to the onion pan and stir with a wooden spoon to make sure every grain is coated in oil. Pour in 10 ounces of the Vin Santo and cook for 3 to 4 minutes, stirring, until the rice has absorbed almost all the wine.

Start to stir in the hot stock, a ladleful at a time, only adding more stock when the last ladleful has been absorbed. Continue to add the stock and stir until the rice is cooked, which will take 20 to 25 minutes.

Remove the risotto from the heat and pour in the remaining Vin Santo. Add in the parsley, butter, and grated Parmesan and stir continuously for 30 seconds, until you have created a creamy texture.

Serve the risotto on warmed serving plates, top with the prosciutto, and garnish with Parmesan shavings.

Roasted Onions in Rosemary and Balsamic Vinegar

Cipolle Borretane SERVES 4

3 tablespoons olive oil

24 boiling onions, peeled

5 tablespoons balsamic vinegar

2 tablespoons honey

1 tablespoon fresh rosemary leaves, stripped from the stalks

Preheat the oven to 350°F.

Heat the olive oil in a large frying pan over medium heat. Add the onions and cook for 5 minutes, stirring continuously with a wooden spoon, until golden all over.

Pour in the vinegar, 4 tablespoons water, and the honey and continue to cook, stirring, for 5 minutes, until the onions are well coated.

Transfer the onions to a roasting pan, stir in the rosemary, and roast in the oven for 15 minutes. Shake the pan at least twice during the roasting time.

Remove the onions from the pan, cool to room temperature, and serve with other antipasti or as a side dish.

Roasted Eggplant with Red Onions and Goat Cheese

Melanzane Arrosto SERVES 4

4 garlic cloves, unpeeled

2 large eggplants, cut into ½-inch-thick slices

2 red onions, peeled and cut into 4 wedges

5 sprigs fresh thyme

6 tablespoons extra virgin olive oil

5 ounces firm goat cheese

¼ cup roughly chopped fresh flat-leaf parsley

Salt and freshly ground black pepper

Preheat the oven to 375°F.

Use the flat side of a knife to squash the unpeeled garlic cloves to release their flavor.

Place the eggplants and the onions in a roasting pan in a single layer. Scatter over the garlic and the thyme. Drizzle with the oil, making sure all the eggplant slices are coated, and season with salt and pepper.

Roast in the middle of the oven for about 30 minutes, or until the eggplants are starting to brown around the edges.

Transfer to a large serving dish and crumble over the goat cheese. Garnish with parsley and serve with a little salad and fresh bread.

Make sure you add the goat cheese and parsley at the last minute before serving.

I have to admit that I'm not a big fan of curry, probably because it contains too many flavors and I'm not used to it, but whenever I have one, I tend to go for something mild and mainly vegetable based. Cauliflower works perfectly with the flavor of the curry paste, and the sweetness of the coconut milk balances the dish beautifully. I've tried this recipe with mixed vegetables and potatoes and it's fantastic.

Cauliflower Curry

Cavolfiore al Curry SERVES 4

3 tablespoons olive oil

2 onions, finely chopped

½ inch piece of ginger, peeled and grated

3 tablespoons curry paste

1 x 14-ounce can coconut milk

14 ounces canned chopped tomatoes

1 head cauliflower, broken into pieces

2 potatoes, peeled and cut into ¾-inch chunks

3 tablespoons freshly squeezed lemon juice

7 ounces spinach leaves, washed

Salt to taste

Heat the oil in a large saucepan and cook the onions for 5 minutes over medium heat until softened, stirring occasionally.

Add the ginger and curry paste and continue to cook for 3 more minutes, stirring continuously.

Pour in the coconut milk and chopped tomatoes and bring to a simmer. Add the cauliflower and potatoes and cook for about 25 minutes, or until the potatoes are softened. Season with salt.

Remove the saucepan from the heat. Add the lemon juice and spinach, cover, and leave for 2 minutes.

Serve hot just as it is or to accompany one of your favorite main courses.

This is the ultimate boys' dish. I absolutely love pulses and I always try to find a different way to cook them. This is a classic for when I have all the boys round to watch *The Godfather* (again!). It gives you a kick, it's tasty and healthy, and it's very filling. You can use any kind of pulse you like or, even better, use a mixture of them to get different colors and textures.

Hot and Spicy Chickpeas

Ceci all'Arrabbiata SERVES 4

2 tablespoons olive oil

1 onion, chopped

2 x 14-ounce cans chickpeas, drained

2 teaspoons dried chile flakes

5 large plum tomatoes, skinned and cut into ½-inch cubes

5 tablespoons chopped fresh flat-leaf parsley

Salt to taste

Put the oil in a medium saucepan over moderate heat and add the onion. Cook for about 8 minutes, until golden brown, stirring constantly.

Add the chickpeas, chile flakes, and tomatoes. Continue to cook for an additional 5 minutes. Stir occasionally to prevent it from sticking.

Just before serving, season with salt to taste, stir in the parsley, and serve hot with your favorite main course.

What can I say... this is definitely a French-style soup. But in my defense, this is such a simple soup to prepare—and I guess the French do come a close second to us Italians (sorry Mr. Novelli) when it comes to cooking. You can substitute a good-quality Cheddar cheese for the Gruyère, and make sure you serve this delicious soup in warmed serving bowls.

Onion Soup with Cheesy Croutons

Zuppa di Cipolle con Crostini al Formaggio SERVES 2

3½ tablespoons salted butter

9 ounces red onions, cut in half and thinly sliced

1 teaspoon brown sugar

6 tablespoons dry white wine

2¼ cups vegetable stock

1 bay leaf

1 small sprig fresh thyme

2 slices country-style bread (preferably 4 to 5 days old)

½ cup freshly grated Gruyère cheese

Salt and freshly ground black pepper

Melt the butter in a medium saucepan and gently cook the onions for about 8 minutes, until softened, stirring occasionally. Add the sugar and continue to cook for an additional 5 minutes, until the onions begin to caramelize.

Pour in the wine and cook for 1 minute, then add the stock, bay leaf, and thyme and simmer for 25 minutes. Stir occasionally and at the end season with salt and pepper.

Meanwhile, preheat the broiler. Place the bread on the broiler and scatter over the cheese. Broil for 2 to 3 minutes, until the cheese is bubbling and golden. Cut each slice into quarters.

Pour the soup into warmed bowls and serve topped with the cheesy croutons.

In the last five or six years there has been a new trend in the south of Italy to create dishes with flavors from the sea and flavors from the mountains combined together. To be completely honest, I wasn't sure if this would work, but after trying it, I am convinced. Please make sure that your clams are fresh and, if you can't find them, substitute mussels. If porcini mushrooms are out of season, use cremini mushrooms.

Pasta with Clams, Rosemary, and Porcini Mushrooms

Linguine Mare e Monti SERVES 4

6 tablespoons olive oil

2 garlic cloves, thinly sliced

1 tablespoon fresh rosemary leaves stripped from the stalks

½ teaspoon crushed dried chiles

7 ounces fresh porcini mushrooms, cleaned and thickly sliced

10 cherry tomatoes, cut in half

2¼ pounds small clams, cleaned (discard any broken ones and those that do not close when tapped firmly)

¼ cup dry white wine

1 pound dried linguine pasta

2 tablespoons chopped fresh flat-leaf parsley

Salt and freshly ground black pepper

Heat the olive oil in a large deep frying pan, add the garlic, rosemary, and the chiles and cook for about 40 seconds over medium heat. Add the mushrooms and cook for an additional 5 minutes, stirring occasionally.

Add the cherry tomatoes, season with salt, and cook for 1 minute. Set aside and keep warm.

Meanwhile, heat a large saucepan over high heat, add the clams and wine, cover with a lid, and cook for 4 minutes, until the clams have opened. (Discard any that remain closed.) Transfer them to a colander for a few seconds, then immediately put them in the frying pan with the mushrooms. Try not to completely drain all the juices from the clams.

Meanwhile, cook the pasta in a large saucepan with plenty of boiling salted water until al dente. Drain thoroughly and pour into the frying pan with the clams and porcini.

Return the frying pan to the heat, sprinkle with the parsley, and toss everything together for a minute. Serve immediately.

In the last couple of years I have received so many letters asking me for a good recipe for a traditional toad in the hole that would be crisp, light, and rise well. One day I woke up with a mission—I was going to come up with a perfect but easy recipe that conquers people's fears about preparing this dish. Of course I couldn't go all the way down the traditional road, as I wanted to add my own touch to this great British classic. Here you have it—enjoy!

Italian Toad in the Hole with Rosemary and Red Onions

SERVES 4

5 tablespoons sunflower oil

8 good-quality Italian sausages

3 red onions, each one cut into 8 wedges

1 tablespoon fresh rosemary leaves, stripped from the stalks

2 cups all-purpose flour

½ teaspoon salt

4 eggs, lightly beaten

1 cup whole milk

Salt and freshly ground black pepper

Preheat the oven to 425°F.

Heat 1 tablespoon of the oil in a large frying pan over medium heat. Start to cook the sausages and the onions with the rosemary for 10 minutes. Turn the sausages and onions regularly until browned. Set aside.

Sift the flour with the salt into a large mixing bowl and make a well in the center. Add the eggs, milk, and a pinch of freshly ground black pepper. Whisk to a smooth batter.

Pour the remaining oil into a medium circular ovenproof dish (about 10 inches in diameter) and place in the middle of the oven for 8 minutes to allow the oil to become very hot.

Arrange the sausages and the onions in the hot oil, then pour over the batter. Bake in the middle of the oven for 25 to 28 minutes, until puffed up and golden.

For maximum effect, simply place the toad in the hole in the center of the table and get your guests to dig in. And don't forget a good bottle of Italian dry red wine to accompany my dish.

I often find myself in a situation where I don't know what to cook for my young boys, and this is always a winner. The comments that I always get from them is that it's very tasty and they absolutely love the crispy topping. You can use any kind of cheese that you like and instead of, or as well as peas, you can add chopped cooked ham. You can also use small shell pasta or bow-shaped pasta.

The Ultimate Macaroni and Cheese

SERVES 4

10 ounces penne or macaroni

1 cup heavy cream

7 ounces sharp cheddar cheese, grated

3½ ounces gorgonzola cheese, cut into small chunks

¼ freshly grated nutmeg

2 mozzarella balls, drained and cut into ½-inch cubes

3 egg yolks

1 cup frozen peas, defrosted

¾ cup freshly grated Parmesan cheese

Salt and freshly ground black pepper

Preheat the oven to 450°F.

Cook the pasta in a large saucepan with plenty of boiling salted water until al dente. Once the pasta is cooked, drain and place back in the same saucepan away from the heat.

Pour in the cream along with the cheddar and gorgonzola cheeses. Return the saucepan to a low heat and use a wooden spoon to mix everything together for 1 minute.

Remove the pan from the heat and add the nutmeg, mozzarella, egg yolks, peas, and half the Parmesan cheese. Season with a little salt, plenty of black pepper, and stir everything together for a good 30 seconds.

Pour the mixture into a shallow-sided ovenproof dish (about 12 x 8 inches), sprinkle the remaining Parmesan on top, and bake in the middle of the oven for about 15 minutes, or until it is bubbling and blistering on top.

Serve immediately with your favorite beer.

It is traditional, especially in northern Italy, to serve lamb with polenta, but in this case I think that mashed potatoes are the ultimate accompaniment—it's impossible to resist the juicy gravy over the mashed potatoes. I know that as an everyday dinner this recipe may seem extravagant, but trust me it is so easy to make and tastes amazing. The secret to get the best results is to use good-quality lamb shanks from your local butcher and a good bottle of red wine. You can substitute cranberry sauce for the red currant jelly.

Roasted Lamb Shank in Red Wine Sauce with Italian Mashed Potatoes

Agnello al Vino Rosso con Purée di Patate SERVES 4

4 lamb shanks

1 carrot, cut into chunks

1 white onion, cut into chunks

3 sprigs fresh rosemary

3 sprigs fresh thyme, plus 4 for garnish

10 whole peppercorns

1 bottle of good-quality red wine

3 red onions, quartered

3 tablespoons red currant jelly

FOR THE MASHED POTATOES

5 large russet or Yukon Gold potatoes, peeled and quartered

⅓ cup whole milk

7 tablespoons salted butter

⅓ cup freshly grated Parmesan cheese

3½ ounces sun-dried tomatoes in oil, drained and finely chopped

Salt and white pepper

Place the lamb shanks, carrot, white onion, herbs, and peppercorns in a large casserole. Pour over the wine, cover, and leave to marinate in a cool place for 5 hours, stirring every hour.

When ready to cook, preheat the oven to 375°F. Place the casserole on the stove and bring to a boil. Cover with the lid and bake in the oven for 2 hours. For the second hour slightly uncover the casserole to allow the sauce to thicken slightly.

Remove the casserole from the oven and transfer the lamb shanks from the cooking liquid into a roasting pan. Spoon over 4 ladlefuls of the liquid to keep the meat moist and add the red onions to the pan.

Return the lamb to the oven and roast for 25 to 30 minutes, or until the meat starts to fall off the bone, basting occasionally.

Strain the cooking liquid into a small saucepan and reduce to half its volume over low heat. Add the red currant jelly and stir until melted.

Meanwhile, prepare the mashed potatoes. Cook the potatoes in plenty of boiling salted water until tender. Drain well and leave to cool slightly.

Press the potatoes through a ricer back into the saucepan, add the milk, and return to low heat. Stir continuously for 3 minutes using a wooden spoon. Add the butter, cheese, and sun-dried tomatoes and continue to stir for an additional 5 minutes. Season with salt and pepper.

Serve a generous spoonful of the mashed potatoes in the center of each serving plate, place the lamb shank on top, and drizzle with the delicious red currant sauce.

Garnish with a sprig of fresh thyme and serve immediately.

For anybody who isn't a big fan of rich tomato sauces, this has to be the perfect pasta recipe if you still want loads of flavor on your plate. I have chosen three different kinds of meats because the pork will give you a great sweet flavor, the beef is good for texture, and the lamb gives you the earthy taste that, combined with the mascarpone cheese, brings the dish together. It's a sauce that you can prepare the day before, and if you have any leftover it is fantastic on a baked potato or rice. You don't have to use all three meats, but try at least to use two and make sure you brown the meat properly before you add the wine.

Rigatoni with White Ragu

Rigatoni al Ragu Bianco SERVES 4

3 tablespoons olive oil

3½ tablespoons butter

1 onion, finely chopped

1 celery stick, finely chopped

1 carrot, finely chopped

3½ ounces smoked diced pancetta

3½ ounces ground pork

3½ ounces ground lamb

7 ounces ground beef

½ cup white wine

1 cup vegetable stock

9 ounces mascarpone cheese

½ teaspoon freshly grated nutmeg

4 tablespoons chopped fresh flat-leaf parsley

1 pound dried rigatoni pasta

1 cup freshly grated Pecorino Romano cheese, to serve

Salt and freshly ground black pepper

Heat the olive oil and the butter in a large saucepan and cook the onion, celery, carrot, and pancetta for about 10 minutes over high heat, until softened and golden.

Add the pork, lamb and beef and mix well to allow the ground meats to crumble. Cook, stirring frequently, for about 10 minutes, or until the meat has browned.

Pour in the wine and cook until evaporated. Season with salt and pepper and add the stock. Lower the heat and simmer, uncovered, for 30 minutes, stirring occasionally to prevent it from sticking.

Mix in the mascarpone cheese, nutmeg, and parsley and allow to rest for 10 minutes.

Meanwhile, cook the pasta in a large saucepan with plenty of boiling salted water until al dente. Once the pasta is cooked, drain thoroughly and immediately add to the sauce. Mix the sauce and the pasta with a wooden spoon over high heat for about 1 minute.

Serve immediately with plenty of grated Pecorino on top.

It's a shame not many people make dishes like this one on a regular basis—I'm sure it's because they think it's difficult. However, every one of my friends who have made this recipe have said how easy it is. You can substitute broccoli for the cauliflower and, if you want to make it more exciting, substitute a selection of wild mushrooms for the carrots.

Italian Vegetable Bake

Sformato di Vegetali SERVES 6

5 ounces carrots, chopped

5 ounces zucchini, chopped

5 ounces cauliflower florets

2 egg whites

¼ cup freshly grated Parmesan cheese

Salt and freshly ground black pepper

FOR THE BECHAMEL SAUCE

2 tablespoons salted butter

¼ cup all-purpose flour

1 cup cold milk

¼ teaspoon grated nutmeg

Preheat the oven to 375°F.

Bring a large saucepan of salted water to a boil and cook the carrots, zucchini, and cauliflower until tender. Drain and allow to cool slightly.

Meanwhile, make the bechamel sauce. Melt the butter in a medium saucepan over medium heat. Stir in the flour and cook for 1 minute. Gradually whisk in the milk, reduce the heat, and cook for 10 minutes, whisking constantly. Once thickened, stir in the nutmeg, season with salt and pepper, and set aside to cool slightly.

Place the vegetables in a food processor and puree until smooth. Pour into a large bowl. Stir the bechamel sauce into the puree.

In a large clean bowl, whisk the egg whites until soft peaks form and fold into the vegetable mixture.

Pour everything into an ovenproof dish and bake in the middle of the oven for 10 minutes. Sprinkle over the Parmesan and return to the oven for an additional 10 minutes.

Serve hot with your favorite salad and accompanied with delicious homemade cheesy breadsticks (see page 142).

This is a recipe that you will find in every Italian cookbook, but mine will guarantee maximum satisfaction! You can use prepared bechamel sauce, but making your own will mean that it tastes that little bit more special and it will give you a feeling of accomplishment. You can substitute ground lamb for ground beef and, once ready and out of the oven, make sure you let it rest for a good 10 minutes, otherwise it will fall apart as you serve it.

The No. 1 Lasagna

Lasagna Numero Uno SERVES 6–8

3 tablespoons olive oil

1 onion, finely chopped

1 large carrot, chopped into ½-inch cubes

1 celery stalk, finely chopped

1 pound ground beef

1 glass Italian dry red wine

14 ounces canned chopped tomatoes

1 tablespoon tomato paste

1 zucchini, chopped into ½-inch cubes

10 basil leaves

9 sheets fresh lasagna (each about 4 x 7 inches)

3½ tablespoons cold salted butter, cut into ¼-inch cubes

Salt and freshly ground black pepper

FOR THE BECHAMEL SAUCE

7 tablespoons salted butter

¾ cup all-purpose flour

3½ cups cold whole milk

1 cup freshly grated Parmesan cheese

¼ freshly grated nutmeg

Heat the olive oil in a large saucepan over medium heat and cook the onion, carrot, and celery for 5 minutes. Add the ground beef and continue to cook for an additional 5 minutes, stirring continuously, until colored all over. Season with salt and pepper and continue to cook for 5 minutes, stirring occasionally.

Pour in the wine, stir well, and continue to cook for about 5 minutes, until the wine has evaporated.

Add the chopped tomatoes, the tomato paste, the zucchini, and basil, lower the heat, and continue to cook for 1 hour, uncovered, until you have a beautiful rich sauce. Stir occasionally. After about 30 minutes, taste for seasoning.

Meanwhile, preheat the oven to 350°F, and make the bechamel sauce. Melt the butter in a large saucepan over medium heat. Stir in the flour and cook for 1 minute. Gradually whisk in the cold milk, reduce the heat, and cook for 10 minutes, whisking constantly. Once thickened, stir in half of the Parmesan cheese with the nutmeg, season, and set aside to cool slightly.

Spread a quarter of the bechamel sauce in the base of a deep 2-quart ovenproof dish. Cover with 3 lasagna sheets, cutting them if necessary to fit the dish. Spread with half the meat sauce, then top with a third of the remaining bechamel sauce. Cover with 3 more sheets of lasagna and then with the remaining meat sauce. Spread over half of the remaining bechamel sauce. Add a final layer of lasagna sheets and gently spread the rest of the bechamel on top, making sure the lasagna sheets are completely covered.

Sprinkle with the remaining Parmesan and scatter over the cubed butter. Grind some black pepper over the whole dish.

Cook on the lowest shelf of the oven for 30 minutes, then place the dish on the middle shelf, raise the oven temperature to 400°F and continue to cook for an additional 15 minutes, until golden and crisp all over.

To tell the truth, I am such a big fan of bread and butter pudding that I had to create my own version of this great dish. The rum with the chocolate is absolutely divine, and with a pinch of cinnamon, it becomes a marriage made in heaven. My only tip for this recipe is to make sure that it rests into the fridge for at least six hours before cooking—this will give you a fantastic soufflé effect when it's ready.

Chocolate and Rum Bread and Butter Pudding

Torta di Pane al Cioccolato SERVES 6

10 slices of good-quality white bread (⅛ inch thick)

5¼ ounces dark chocolate (70 percent cocoa solids)

2 cups heavy cream

¼ cup dark rum

5½ tablespoons salted butter

½ cup superfine sugar

Pinch of cinnamon

3 eggs

Chilled heavy cream, to serve

Remove the crusts from the bread and cut each slice into 4 triangles.

Place the chocolate, cream, rum, butter, sugar, and cinnamon in a large bowl set over a saucepan with simmering water. Be careful not to let the bowl touch the water. Once the butter and chocolate have melted and the sugar is completely dissolved, remove the bowl from the heat and stir to amalgamate the ingredients.

In a separate bowl, whisk the eggs and then pour the chocolate mixture over them and whisk again to blend everything together.

Lightly butter a shallow ovenproof dish measuring about 7 x 10 x 2 inches.

Pour about a ½-inch layer of chocolate mixture into the base of the dish and arrange half the bread triangles over the chocolate in overlapping rows.

Pour half the remaining chocolate over the bread and arrange the rest of the triangles over that, finishing off with a layer of chocolate. Press the bread gently down so that it is evenly covered with the liquid. Leave to cool.

Cover the dish with plastic wrap and place in the fridge for at least 6 hours.

Preheat the oven to 350°F.

Remove the plastic wrap and bake the pudding in the middle of the oven for 35 minutes—the top will be crunchy and the inside still soft and squidgy.

Remove from the oven, leave to relax for about 5 minutes, and serve with plenty of chilled heavy cream poured all over.

Torta di Pane al Cioccolato

SERVES
6

After having such great feedback from my Plum and Limoncello Tart in my previous book, *Fantastico*, I wanted to create something similar for you citrus lovers out there—I'm sure you'll like this one just as much. I have also tried the same recipe with fresh papaya, and it's been a great success. Make sure you always serve the tart at room temperature and never straight from the fridge.

The Best Lemon and Mango Tart

Torta di Limoni e Mango SERVES 6–8

1½ cups all-purpose flour

½ teaspoon salt

9 tablespoons chilled butter, diced

½ cup ground almonds

2 tablespoons confectioners' sugar, plus extra for dusting

2 egg yolks

1 egg white, beaten

FOR THE FILLING

1 cup superfine sugar

4 eggs

½ cup heavy cream

Grated zest and juice of 2 lemons

2 mangoes, peeled and cut into ¼-inch cubes

To make the pastry, place the flour, salt, butter, ground almonds, and confectioners' sugar in a food processor and process to make fine crumbs. Add 2 tablespoons cold water and the egg yolks and pulse until the mixture comes together to make a firm but moist dough. Wrap in plastc wrap and chill for 30 minutes.

Turn out the pastry onto a floured surface and lightly shape into a ball. Roll out and use to line an 8-inch fluted flan pan. Chill for at least 30 minutes.

Preheat the oven to 375°F.

Line the pastry case with wax paper, fill with baking beans, and bake in the middle of the oven for 10 minutes. Lift out the paper, return to the oven, and continue to bake for an additional 5 minutes, until the pastry is dry. Brush the pastry with the beaten egg white and return to the oven for another 5 minutes, until the egg white has dried and the pastry is shiny. (Using egg white prevents the pastry from getting soggy once the filling is poured in.)

Reduce the oven temperature to 300°F.

To make the filling, beat the superfine sugar and eggs until foamy. Beat in the cream with the lemon zest and juice. Arrange the mango cubes on the bottom of the empty tart case and carefully pour over the lemon mixture.

Bake in the middle of the oven for 35 to 40 minutes until just set. (Don't worry if the filling is wobbly in the center, as it will set as it cools.)

Leave to cool, then slip it out of the pan and dust with plenty of confectioners' sugar. Serve at room temperature with crème fraîche.

When you have guests for dinner, have you ever felt that after making an effort on the appetizer and main course, you really can't be bothered to make a dessert? The answer to this dilemma is simple—either go buy a prepared one or use this recipe, because it's the easiest but tastiest dessert to prepare. You can use any berries that you like and, instead of whiskey, try a good brandy.

Strawberries and Raspberries Layered with Whiskey Cream

Fragole e Lamponi SERVES 6

9 ounces strawberries, hulled and halved

9 ounces raspberries

3 tablespoons whiskey

2 tablespoons rolled oats

2 tablespoons slivered almonds

1½ cups heavy cream

2 tablespoons honey

Carefully mix together the strawberries and raspberries in a large bowl. Pour in 2 tablespoons of the whiskey, toss the fruit to mix, and leave to marinate for about 5 minutes. You will want to reserve a few of the marinated berries for decoration.

Meanwhile, pan-roast the oats and almonds in a small frying pan over medium heat for about 5 minutes. Once golden and toasted, set aside to cool.

Use an electric mixer to whip the cream into soft peaks. Pour in the honey and the remaining whiskey and whip for an additonal 5 seconds, until combined.

Fold half the cooled oats and almonds into the mixture.

Layer the berries and cream evenly into 6 tall dessert glasses, ending with the cream. Cover the glasses with plastic wrap and refrigerate for 2 hours.

To serve, remove the plastic wrap, sprinkle with the remaining oats and almonds, and decorate with the reserved berries.

Facile Facile

Easy but impressive recipes

Facile in Italian means easy, and this is exactly

what you are going to get in this chapter. I wanted to create dishes that look very impressive but are made effortlessly and with few ingredients. This chapter shows off what Italian food is all about—colors, flavors, and great textures. The main reason why I decided to write "Facile Facile"- is because I know that today's lifestyle gives us very little time to spend in the kitchen. However, we all love to entertain, have friends over, and show off our cooking ability, so this chapter fits these criteria— and there is very little washing up to do too!

If you love eggs and you're looking for something full of flavor, this is an exciting dish to try. It's very colorful and extremely easy to prepare. It is also a wonderful dish to eat cold or the day after as a packed lunch for the office. Trust me, your colleagues will be so jealous! You can substitute goat cheese for the feta and, if you are not a big fan of sun-dried tomatoes, use fresh tomatoes instead.

Baked Omelette with Sun-dried Tomatoes, Arugula, and Feta Cheese

Frittata SERVES 6

3 tablespoons extra virgin olive oil

9 ounces leeks, trimmed and thinly sliced

3½ ounces arugula leaves

3½ ounces spinach

3½ ounces kale, shredded

8 large eggs

3 tablespoons chopped fresh mint leaves

5½ ounces Greek feta cheese, crumbled

¼ cup freshly grated Parmesan cheese

2 ounces sun-dried tomatoes in oil, drained and thinly sliced

Salt and freshly ground black pepper

Preheat the oven to 325°F.

Heat the oil in a large saucepan over medium heat and cook the leeks for 10 minutes, until soft. Add the arugula, spinach, and kale to the pan and continue to cook for an additional 4 to 5 minutes, until they have wilted down. Transfer the mixture to a large bowl and leave to cool slightly.

Break the eggs into the bowl with the greens and add the mint, feta, Parmesan, and sun-dried tomatoes. Season with salt and pepper and mix well.

Oil a shallow 8-inch cake pan, preferably nonstick. Pour in the mixture and bake in the middle of the oven for about 40 minutes, or until just set.

Allow the frittata to rest for 3 minutes before slicing. Serve with a beautiful tomato salad.

The one thing that I have to say about this recipe is that it looks spectacular. I love the combination of parsley and peas, and the fact that in less than 20 minutes you will have a soup that you will never forget. I often make it for dinner with some warm crusty bread and it's really filling. If fresh peas aren't available, you can always use good-quality frozen ones, but always, always, always use fresh flat-leaf parsley.

Fresh Pea and Parsley Soup

Zuppa di Piselli e Prezzemolo SERVES 4

2 tablespoons butter

4 shallots, finely chopped

1¾ pounds fresh peas

1 vegetable bouillon cube

2 tablespoons chopped fresh flat-leaf parsley

7 tablespoons heavy cream

Salt and white pepper

Melt the butter in a large saucepan over medium heat and cook the shallots for 5 minutes, stirring occasionally. Add the peas with 2¾ cups water and the bouillon cube. Bring to a boil, then turn down the heat, add the parsley, and simmer, covered, for about 12 minutes for young peas and up to 18 minutes for larger or older peas. Stir occasionally.

When the peas are tender, ladle them into a food processor or blender with a little of the cooking liquid. Purée until smooth.

Return the soup to the pan, pour in half the cream, season with salt and pepper, and reheat without boiling.

Serve in warm bowls garnished with a drizzle of the remaining cream.

I have to admit that I'm not a great lover of beets, probably because I don't particularly like sweet and sour together. This, however, is one of the few ways that I will eat beets because it works beautifully with the smoked salmon. If you are a beet virgin—here you go, this is the one to try. Make sure you cook the rostis until they are very crisp.

Beet Rosti with Smoked Salmon and Horseradish Cream

Crocchette di Barbabietola e Salmone SERVES 4

2 large potatoes (about 1 pound), unpeeled

1 beet, peeled and coarsely grated

1 garlic clove, crushed

5 tablespoons olive oil

4 slices good-quality smoked salmon

1 lime, cut into 4 wedges

FOR THE HORSERADISH CREAM

3½ ounces mascarpone cheese

Juice of ½ lime

2 tablespoons horseradish sauce

Salt and freshly ground black pepper

Fresh dill sprigs to garnish

Put the potatoes into a large saucepan, cover with cold water, and bring to a boil. Cook for 12 minutes, then drain and leave to cool.

Peel the cooled potatoes and grate into a large bowl. Add the beet and garlic, season with salt and pepper and mix well.

Divide and mold the mixture into 4 patties. Leave to chill in the fridge for 40 to 60 minutes.

Meanwhile, mix the mascarpone, lime juice, and horseradish in a bowl. Season with salt and plenty of black pepper.

Heat the oil in a frying pan and cook the rostis for about 5 minutes on each side, until crisp and golden all over. Remove and drain on paper towels.

Place a hot rosti on each serving plate topped with some smoked salmon, a dollop of horseradish cream, and a sprig of dill. Place a wedge of lime on the side and serve immediately.

If you like traditional pesto made with basil, oil, and pine nuts, you will absolutely love my parsley and caper pesto. This is one of my signature dishes that never fails to impress people and, funnily enough, like all the best dishes in the world, it's very simple to prepare. Please make sure that your pasta is al dente and, once the pasta is mixed into the sauce, you must serve immediately otherwise it will get sticky and soggy. Buon Appetito!

Pasta with Walnut and Caper Pesto

Tagliolini al Pesto di Noci e Capperi SERVES 4

FOR THE PESTO

2 garlic cloves, chopped

3 ounces walnut halves, chopped

2 tablespoons salted capers, rinsed and chopped

2 ounces fresh flat-leaf parsley, chopped

¾ cup extra virgin olive oil

3½ tablespoons salted butter, softened

5 tablespoons freshly grated Pecorino Romano cheese

Salt and freshly ground black pepper

1 pound tagliolini (fresh or dried)

Place the garlic, walnuts, capers, and a little salt in a mortar and pestle and pound until broken up. Add the parsley and continue to pound until you create a paste. (If you don't have a mortar and pestle, briefly pulse the ingredients in a food processor to a rough pesto.)

Transfer the mixture into a bowl and gradually mix in the oil until creamy and thick. Beat in the butter and season with pepper. Finally, beat in the Pecorino.

Meanwhile, cook the pasta in a large saucepan in plenty of boiling salted water until al dente. Drain and return to the pan off the heat.

Pour the pesto in the pan and use a wooden spoon to fold the pesto into the pasta for at least 30 seconds to make sure the pasta is well dressed. If you like, sprinkle with a little extra grated Pecorino. Serve immediately with a cold beer.

SERVES
4

This recipe reminds me of Rome, especially around Easter time, because it seems to me that every Roman eats fava beans with Pecorino cheese during the festive season. I personally think that it's a brilliant salad combination because I adore the saltiness of the speck with the sweetness of the fava beans. A simple, tasty dish that can be eaten on its own, or to accompany any meat main course.

Pecorino and Fava Bean Salad with Speck

Insalata di Fave, Pecorino e Speck SERVES 4

¾ pound fresh fava beans

6 small celery stalks, sliced into 2-inch long matchsticks

10 mint leaves, roughly sliced

3½ ounces arugula leaves

5 tablespoons extra virgin olive oil

Juice of 1 small lemon

5½ ounces Pecorino Romano cheese, shaved

Salt and freshly ground black pepper

12 slices speck (or prosciutto)

Bring a large saucepan of water to a boil and cook the fava beans for no longer than 2 minutes. Drain, rinse in cold water, and leave to cool.

Put the beans, celery, mint, and arugula leaves in a large bowl. Make a dressing by pouring the oil and lemon juice into a small bowl, season with salt and pepper, and whisk until it begins to thicken slightly. Pour the dressing over the salad and toss to make sure all the ingredients are well coated.

Distribute the salad among four serving plates and fold 3 slices of speck on top of each serving. Scatter the Pecorino shavings over the salads and serve immediately with good, warm country-style bread.

If you asked me the three things I miss most about Italy, my answer would be very simple: the sun, good soccer, and simple and tasty dishes like this one. Unfortunately, I don't see enough restaurants serving fresh fish like this, and this is such a shame because I'm sure that everybody would love it. This way of marinating and cooking fish in lemon juice is also a traditional Mexican style that relies completely on fresh and good-quality ingredients.

Sea Bass Carpaccio with Chiles and Cherry Tomatoes

Carpaccio di Spigola e Pomodorini di Collina SERVES 4 AS AN APPETIZER

2¼ pounds whole sea bass (or salmon if you prefer), filleted

10 cherry tomatoes, halved

5 tablespoons freshly squeezed lemon juice

3 tablespoons extra virgin olive oil

⅛ teaspoon dried chile flakes

3 tablespoons fresh oregano leaves

Salt

Place the sea bass fillets on a cutting board, skin side down. Use a long-bladed sharp knife to cut as finely as you can along the length of the fillets. Discard the skin.

Place the fillets, side by side, on a large cold serving plate. Squeeze the juice and the pulp from the halved tomatoes over the fish and scatter the skins on top. Drizzle with the lemon juice and oil. Season with a little salt and the chile flakes and scatter with the oregano leaves.

Cover the plate with plastic wrap and chill for about 1 hour, until the fish is opaque.

Serve with some warm crusty bread of your choice.

Stuffed Roasted Tomatoes with Goat Cheese and Mozzarella

Pomodori Imbottiti al Formaggio SERVES 6

6 beefsteak tomatoes

4-ounce ball mozzarella cheese, drained and finely chopped

2 tablespoons crushed walnuts

6 ounces goat cheese, rind removed

2 tablespoons chopped fresh basil

6 thick slices white bread

Extra virgin olive oil, for drizzling

Salt and freshly ground black pepper

Preheat the oven to 375°F.

Using a sharp knife, cut a thin slice from the bottom of each tomato, so that the base is flat and the tomatoes won't topple over, and discard. Cut a ½-inch slice from the top of the tomato, but do not discard. Carefully scoop out the seeds and most of the pulp with a teaspoon, keeping the tomato shells whole.

Mix together the mozzarella, walnuts, goat cheese, and basil. Season with salt and pepper and spoon into the tomato shells. Replace the tomato lid.

Use a 3-inch-round pastry cutter to stamp out 6 rounds from the bread slices and toast on both sides. Set aside.

Place the tomatoes on a lightly oiled baking sheet and bake in the middle of the oven for about 20 minutes, just until the cheese mixture looks melted and golden (you don't want the tomatoes to be too soft). Serve immediately, on top of the toasted bread, with a little drizzle of extra virgin olive oil on top.

Lentils and Nuts with Chive and Sherry Vinegar Dressing

Lenticchie e Noci con Erba Cipollina SERVES 4

14 ounces canned green lentils

3 tablespoons walnuts, chopped

2 tablespoons pine nuts, toasted

2 tablespoons chopped hazelnuts

3 tablespoons chopped fresh chives

3 tablespoons extra virgin olive oil

2 tablespoons sherry vinegar

Salt and white pepper

Drain and rinse the lentils under cold water and place in a large bowl. Add the nuts and chives and mix everything together.

Pour in the oil and vinegar and season with salt and pepper. Toss well and serve with your favorite main course or as a starter with some warm crusty bread.

In my hometown, Torre del Greco, the words "scue scue" mean something done "quickly quickly." This has to be the most tasty, colorful, and easy salad that you will ever prepare, and it will make a good brunch alternative or an easy dinner for any day of the week. My tip is to dress the salad just before serving, otherwise you will cook the lettuce and everything will get dark and soggy.

Quick Ham and Emmental Salad with Dijon Mustard Dressing

Insalata Scue' Scue' SERVES 4

1 head iceberg lettuce, leaves separated and roughly torn

2 ounces radicchio leaves

3 ounces Emmental cheese, grated

5½ ounces ham, cut into ⅛-inch cubes

1 ripe avocado, cut into big chunks

7 ounces canned corn, drained

4 eggs, boiled for 6 minutes, peeled, and quartered

FOR THE DRESSING

4 tablespoons extra virgin olive oil

1 tablespoon red wine vinegar

1 teaspoon Dijon mustard

Salt and freshly ground black pepper

First make the dressing by whisking together the oil, vinegar, and mustard in a small bowl and season with salt and pepper.

Place the torn lettuce leaves in a large bowl with the radicchio leaves. Add the cheese, ham, avocado, and corn. Pour in the dressing and toss.

Divide the salad among 4 serving plates and arrange 4 wedges of egg on top.

Serve immediately as an appetizer or brunch with some warm crusty bread.

I don't about know you, but sometimes I get bored of always having potatoes with my main meal. I created this in order to still have a substantial side dish, but with more exciting colors and flavors. Try this recipe with pumpkin when it is in season, and you can use Parmesan cheese instead of Pecorino.

Roasted Squash with Chiles and Sage Crumbs

Zucca al Forno con Peperoncino e Salvia SERVES 6

3½ ounces fresh breadcrumbs

6 tablespoons olive oil

2 butternut squash, unpeeled, seeds and fibers removed, cut into thin wedges

1 medium hot red chile, seeded and sliced

2 garlic cloves, sliced

10 whole fresh sage leaves

¼ cup freshly grated Pecorino Sardo

Salt and freshly ground black pepper

Preheat the oven to 400°F.

Put the breadcrumbs in a bowl and drizzle over half the oil. Season with salt and pepper and toss together.

Place the squash in a roasting pan, drizzle with the remaining oil, and sprinkle with the chile, garlic, and sage. Season with salt.

Sprinkle over the breadcrumbs and cheese and bake in the middle of the oven for about 40 to 45 minutes, until tender and golden. Serve hot.

I'm going to dedicate this recipe to my sister Marcella because every time she comes to visit me in London, she always asks me to prepare it. I think the main reason for this is because we don't get good-quality potatoes in Italy; also the flavor of the chives and the cheeses work wonderfully together. If you want, add a couple of teaspoons of spicy mustard.

Cheesy Mashed Potatoes with Chives

Puree di Patate con Erba Cipollina SERVES 4

2¼ pounds potatoes, peeled and quartered

½ cup whole milk

¾ cup freshly grated Parmesan cheese

½ cup freshly grated cheddar cheese

7 tablespoons salted butter

5 tablespoons finely chopped fresh chives

Salt and white pepper

Put the potatoes in a large saucepan, cover with cold water, and bring to a boil. Cook until tender. Drain and mash in the saucepan. Return the pan to low heat and, using a wooden spoon, stir in the milk, then beat to a creamy texture.

Add the cheeses, butter, and chives, season and stir for an additional 3 minutes over a low heat until the cheeses are completely melted; you want to create a beautiful creamy texture. Serve immediately.

Pasta is definitely the ultimate Italian fast food. I don't think I've ever met anyone who doesn't like a plate of good pasta. I often make white sauce with mascarpone cheese, and this is without doubt one of my top five pasta dishes. The crispness of the pancetta with the sweet peas and the cheese is an explosion of taste. You can substitute fusilli for the tagliatelle or rigatoni and remember: put the pasta into the sauce, never the sauce on top of the pasta!

Pasta with Mushrooms, Peas, and Mascarpone

Tagliatelle al Mascarpone SERVES 4

1 tablespoon olive oil

3½ tablespoons salted butter

3½ ounces pancetta, cubed

5½ ounces button mushrooms, quartered

¾ cup defrosted frozen or fresh peas

9 ounces mascarpone cheese

1 pound fresh tagliatelle

½ cup freshly grated Parmesan cheese

Salt and freshly ground black pepper

Heat the oil and butter together in a large frying pan over medium heat. Add the pancetta and a pinch of black pepper and cook for about 3 minutes, until golden.

Add the mushrooms and peas and continue to cook for 8 minutes, stirring occasionally.

Stir in the mascarpone cheese and remove the pan from the heat.

Meanwhile, cook the pasta in a large saucepan with plenty of boiling salted water (allow at least 3 quarts water) until al dente.

Once the pasta is cooked, drain thoroughly and add to the frying pan with the sauce.

Put the pan back on the heat, sprinkle half of the Parmesan over the pasta, and toss everything together for a good minute.

Serve immediately, sprinkled with the remaining grated Parmesan.

The original topping for a traditional Neapolitan pizza is tomato, garlic, oregano, and extra virgin olive oil. The mozzarella was added by a Neapolitan pizza guy who wanted to impress a queen called Margherita. Since then it's become probably the most renowned and popular pizza in the world! As you can see I have added a few extra ingredients to make it more exciting so you can do exactly the same as long as it's not pineapple – what is that all about?

Pizza Vesuvio

MAKES 2 PIZZAS

FOR THE DOUGH

Pinch of salt

1 teaspoon dried yeast

½ cup warm water

1¼ cups bread flour, plus extra for dusting

1 tablespoon extra virgin olive oil, plus extra for greasing

FOR THE TOPPING

14 ounces fresh tomato sauce (sieved tomatoes)

2 mozzarella balls, cut into pieces (do not use buffalo mozzarella because it is too milky and will make the dough soggy)

12 slices good-quality Italian salami

3½ ounces pitted Kalamata black olives, halved

4 tablespoons extra virgin olive oil

¼ cup freshly grated Parmesan cheese

10 fresh basil leaves

Salt and freshly ground black pepper

To make the dough, mix together the salt, yeast, and water in a pitcher. Sift the flour into a large bowl, make a well in the center, and add the yeast mixture along with the olive oil. Use a wooden spoon to mix everything together to create a wet dough.

Turn out the dough onto a clean well-floured surface and work it with your hands for about 5 minutes, until smooth and elastic. Place in a bowl and cover with a dish towel. Leave in a warm place to rest for at least 30 minutes or until the dough almost doubles in size.

Preheat the oven to 425°F.

Once rested, turn out the dough onto a floured surface and divide it into two. Use your hands (or a rolling pin) to push each out from the center, creating two round discs about 10 inches in diameter. Place the pizza bases on two oiled baking sheets.

Spread the tomato sauce over the pizza dough using a tablespoon and season with salt and pepper. Divide the mozzarella, salami, and olives between the pizzas and drizzle with the extra virgin olive oil. Bake in the middle of the oven for about 20 minutes, or until golden and browned. Two minutes before the end of the cooking time sprinkle the pizzas with Parmesan and scatter the basil leaves on top.

Serve hot and enjoy with a cold beer.

This is a great recipe that I learned in the town of Sorrento about twenty years ago when I was a student. The secret for this recipe is to buy good-quality lamb and also good-quality juicy lemons. I absolutely adore lamb, especially when it's slow-cooked and falling off the bone. Ask your butcher to cut the shoulder of lamb through the bone into 4 large chunks. A fantastic recipe that you can prepare in advance and is even better if served the next day.

Slow-Roasted Shoulder of Lamb with Lemon Potatoes

Agnello e Patate al Forno all'Oregano e Limone SERVES 4

3½ pounds shoulder of lamb

3½ pounds red potatoes, peeled and cut into 2-inch chunks

10 garlic cloves, unpeeled

1 tablespoon dried oregano

2 tablespoons fresh marjoram leaves

2 tablespoons fresh rosemary leaves, stripped from the stalk

3 bay leaves

5 tablespoons extra virgin olive oil

Juice of 2 large lemons

Salt and freshly ground black pepper

Preheat the oven to 375°F.

Place the meat, potatoes, and garlic in a large ovenproof casserole dish. Sprinkle in all the herbs and pour in the olive oil, lemon juice, and ½ cup cold water.

Season with plenty of salt and pepper and mix well together (try to nestle the pieces of meat down among the potatoes.) Cover the casserole dish with foil and a well-fitting lid.

Bake in the middle of the oven for 3 hours, until the meat is falling off the bone. Check after about 2 hours to see whether it needs a little more water.

At the end of cooking, let the casserole rest for 10 minutes out of the oven with the lid off.

Serve with plain rice or a fresh salad of your choice.

Originally I wanted to put this recipe in the *Romantico* chapter because it's delicate and very pretty, but then considering how easy it is to prepare, I put it here. I am obsessed with veal, and this has to be one of my favorite ways to cook it. The sharpness of the lemon with the sweetness of veal is *buonissimo!* My tip is to only use fresh sage leaves and never the dried ones from the jars and to open a good bottle of cold Italian white wine to serve with this dish.

Veal with Butter, Sage, and Lemon Sauce

Scaloppine di Vitello al Limone SERVES 4

3 lemons

¼ cup all-purpose flour, for dusting

4 x 6-ounce thinly sliced veal scaloppine

4 tablespoons salted butter

3 tablespoons extra virgin olive oil

7 tablespoons dry white wine

5 fresh sage leaves, finely sliced

Salt and freshly ground black pepper

Peel 1 lemon and slice into 8 thin slices, without any pith.

Spread the flour on a flat plate, season with salt and pepper, and mix.

Dust the veal in the seasoned flour, shaking off any excess.

Melt the butter in a large frying pan over medium heat, then pour in the oil. When it is hot, lay the scaloppine in the pan with the lemon slices and cook for 2 minutes on each side.

Pour in the juice from 1½ lemons and the wine and shake the pan constantly—this will make the sauce creamy. Remove the veal and the lemon slices and arrange on a warm serving plate.

Add the sage to the sauce, give it a good shake, and immediately pour over the scaloppine.

Serve with a chilled glass of good white Italian wine.

This is my grandmother nonna Assunta's signature dish. She knows very well that every time I go to see her I expect to see these beautiful meatballs on a plate even if I go there for breakfast. Make sure you use plenty of freshly grated Parmesan cheese, and once the meatballs are ready you can toss some freshly cooked spaghetti with it.

Neapolitan Spicy Meatballs in Tomato Sauce

Polpette alla Napoletana SERVES 4

18 ounces ground beef

3½ ounces salami Napoli, chopped

3 garlic cloves, crushed

2¾ ounces fresh white breadcrumbs

1 teaspoon dried chile flakes

3 tablespoons chopped fresh flat-leaf parsley

¾ cup freshly grated Parmesan cheese

1 egg

3 pounds tomato sauce (sieved tomatoes)

10 fresh basil leaves

4 tablespoons olive oil

Salt and white pepper

Combine the ground beef, salami, garlic, breadcrumbs, chile flakes, parsley, and Parmesan in a large bowl. Season with salt and break in the egg. Mix all the ingredients thoroughly with your hands, then shape into 8 balls. Place on a plate and leave in the fridge for 20 minutes.

Meanwhile, pour the tomato sauce into a large saucepan and place over medium heat. Season with salt and pepper, add the basil leaves, bring to a boil, then remove from the heat.

Heat the oil in a large frying pan and cook the meatballs for about 5 minutes, until golden brown all over.

Place the meatballs in the tomato sauce and continue to cook over low heat for 1 hour with the pan half covered. Stir occasionally and, if the sauce gets too thick, add a little water.

Serve 2 meatballs per person with the sauce and some freshly cooked pasta or plain rice.

If you decide to prepare a fishy appetizer and want to follow it with a meat dish, the problem that you will find is that during the main course you will still be able to taste the fish. Well, I have the solution—serve my granita just after the starter and it will cleanse your palate ready for the main course. A fantastic, refreshing sorbet that is also great on a hot day with a barbecue.

Limoncello and Lime Granita

Granita al Limoncello SERVES 4

Zest and juice of
2 limes

3½ cups cold water

⅛ cup superfine
sugar

1 cup Limoncello
liqueur

Place the lime juice in a medium saucepan with the cold water. Add the sugar and half the lime zest and gently heat until the sugar has dissolved, stirring occasionally.

Remove from the heat, mix in the Limoncello, and leave to cool.

Pour the cooled mixture into a flat freezerproof container and freeze until crystals form around the edges (about 30 minutes, depending on your freezer). At this point, stir the mixture vigorously with a fork, then put it back in the freezer.

Repeat this process every 20 minutes over the next few hours, until no liquid remains in the container. The consistency you're after is just crunchy with broken crystals of ice.

Serve the granita in tall glasses, decorated with the remaining lime zest.

Not only do my boys Rocco and Luciano love to eat this dessert, but they also love to help me make it. This tiramisu was especially designed for children so of course there is no alcohol involved, but if you want a grown-up version, you can always add four or five tablespoons of Amaretto liqueur into the cream mixture. Remember not to soak the cookies too much or they will get too soggy, and make sure your chocolate is cold.

Chocolate Tiramisu

Tiramisu alla Rocco SERVES 4

6 tablespoons cocoa

1 cup low-fat milk

1 cup heavy cream

9 ounces mascarpone cheese

3 tablespoons superfine sugar

1 teaspoon vanilla extract

20 Savoiardi cookies (lady fingers)

4 chocolate flakes to decorate

Put the drinking chocolate and milk in a medium saucepan over medium heat, stirring occasionally. When the chocolate has dissolved, pour into a bowl and leave to cool.

Whip the cream in a large bowl until soft peaks form. Add the mascarpone cheese, sugar, and vanilla extract and whip for an additional 10 seconds, until everything is combined.

You will need four glass dessert dishes, about 3 inches in diameter and 2½ inches deep.

Dip 8 Savoiardi cookies into the chocolate milk for 2 seconds on each side and place 2 fingers on the base of each dish. (Break the cookies to make sure the bottom of the dish is covered.)

Divide the mascarpone cream among the four dishes to cover the fingers.

Dip the remaining cookies in the chocolate and this time place 3 cookies on top of the cream in each dish. Finish by smothering the remaining cream over the sponge fingers. Cover each dish with plastic wrap and chill for 1 hour.

To serve, remove the plastic wrap and sprinkle the chocolate flakes over each tiramisu.

If you take away the Amaretto liqueur from this recipe, it will be perfect for when you have kids coming over. I guarantee you that everyone is going to love these crispy, chocolatey, and chewy little crunchy bars that go perfectly with a cup of tea or, for the adults, a good brandy. Made sure you use a good-quality chocolate and that the pistachios are not salted.

Chocolate and Pistachio Crunch Bars

Bocconcini di Cioccolato e Pistacchio SERVES 8 (MAKES 24 PIECES)

3½ tablespoons salted butter

10¼ ounces good-quality dark chocolate (70 percent cocoa solids), broken into pieces

3 tablespoons dark corn syrup

3 tablespoons Amaretto liqueur

7 ounces graham crackers

3 ounces mini marshmallows

3 ounces crushed pistachios

Confectioners' sugar, for dusting

Place the butter, chocolate, syrup, and Amaretto liqueur in a heavy-bottom saucepan and gently heat until melted. Pour ¼ cup of the mixture out of the pan and set aside.

Place the graham crackers in a large bowl and crush into rough crumbs with your hands. Fold into the chocolate mixture in the saucepan, along with the marshmallows and pistachios.

Pour the mixture into an aluminum tray measuring about 10 inches square, and use a spatula to flatten as best you can. Pour over the reserved melted chocolate and smooth the top.

Cover with plastic wrap and refrigerate for about 3 hours or overnight.

To serve, push out the cake on a cutting board and cut into 24 fingers. Dust with confectioners' sugar and place on a large serving dish.

Buonissimo with a good cup of your favorite tea.

I know that this may sound very strange to you, using black pepper in a white chocolate mousse, but believe you me, this is a dessert that all your friends will talk about. This recipe has been designed specifically for this chapter; it's easy, very tasty, and definitely has the wow factor, but make sure you use a good-quality chocolate. You can also serve it straight from the freezer like a semifreddo.

White Chocolate Mousse with Black Pepper and Fresh Mint

Mousse di Cioccolato Bianco e Pepe Nero SERVES 6

10 ounces white chocolate, broken into pieces

½ cup heavy cream

1 tablespoon freshly ground black pepper

12 fresh mint leaves (6 thinly sliced, 6 reserved for decoration)

Put the chocolate in a heatproof bowl and place over a pan of simmering water to melt. Make sure the base of the bowl does not touch the water. When the chocolate has melted, stand the bowl on a cold surface to cool down slightly.

Pour the cream into a large bowl and beat until soft peaks form.

Place 2 tablespoons of cream in the melted chocolate and gently fold together, then fold the chocolate mixture into the rest of the cream. At the end, gently fold in the black pepper and chopped mint.

Divide the mixture among six tall champagne glasses (capacity of about 3 ounces).

Chill in the fridge for about 20 minutes, then serve decorated with the reserved mint leaves.

SERVES
6

Salute

Party food for sharing

Whenever I am in Italy and everyone clinks

glasses and shouts out *salute* (cheers), I know that it's party time.
I personally believe that when there is a special occasion, people shouldn't
spend too much time in the kitchen preparing things that will take them
away from their guests. So here I've created recipes that you can
definitely prepare ahead, leaving you plenty of time to party. Take, for
example, my semifreddo all'amaretto, a fantastic dessert that, prepared
the day before, will taste ten times better. Remember, a great party
always needs a good drink, so use the one I've suggested to impress your
friends. One important tip I can give you is to try the recipe you choose
for your party at least once before the big day to make sure that it's
going to work perfectly.

Campari Served with Parmesan Crisps

Marco on the Rock SERVES 4

½ cup Campari

1 cup orange juice

1 cup tomato juice

TO SERVE

Ice cubes

Fine strips of
cucumber

FOR THE CRISPS

½ cup freshly grated
Parmesan cheese

Leaves from 4 fresh
thyme sprigs

First, prepare the crisps. Preheat the oven to 350°F. Make 8 small heaps of the grated Parmesan on a baking sheet, spaced about ¾ inch apart. Sprinkle the thyme over the cheese piles. Bake in the oven for 4 to 5 minutes until melted, lacy, and golden. Remove from the oven and immediately lay each crisp on a rolling pin to curve it slightly. Set aside to cool.

Meanwhile, mix together the Campari, orange juice, and tomato juice in a large pitcher. Place several ice cubes in 4 glasses, then pour over the mixed Campari. Decorate the glass with the cucumber strips and enjoy with your Parmesan crisps.

Cheesy Breadsticks with Pecorino Cheese and Thyme

Grissini al Pecorino MAKES 35–40

¾ ounce dried yeast

1 cup tepid milk

6 cups bread flour,
plus extra for
dusting

4 teaspoons salt

⅔ cups freshly
grated Pecorino
cheese

7 tablespoons salted
butter, at room
temperature

Extra virgin olive
oil, for greasing

2 tablespoons finely
chopped fresh thyme
leaves, stripped from
the sprigs

Mix the yeast in a glass with 3 tablespoons of the milk, stir well, and leave to rest for 10 minutes.

Stir the flour, salt, and cheese together in a large bowl. Rub in the butter using your fingertips until the mixture resembles breadcrumbs. Stir in the yeast mixture and gradually incorporate the remaining milk to form a soft dough.

Turn out the dough onto a floured surface and knead for about 10 minutes, until the dough is soft and elastic.

Lightly oil a large bowl and place the dough in it. Drizzle the top with a little more oil and cover with plastic wrap. Leave in a warm place for about 1 hour, until nearly doubled in size.

Once the dough is ready, knock it back by punching it, then turn out on a clean unfloured surface. Cut into 8 pieces, roll out, then cut each into sausage shapes about ⅛ inch thick and the length of a baking sheet. Sprinkle over the chopped thyme and divide them between 2 baking sheets. Leave to rest for 15 minutes in a warm place. Meanwhile, preheat the oven to 450°F.

Bake the breadsticks in the middle of the oven for about 15 minutes, until golden. Leave to cool on a wire rack. Serve them warm or cold.

I designed this recipe on the day that my son Luciano turned six. I remember my wife saying that the food she was going to prepare was a little boring, so she asked me to come up with something more exciting. This turned out to be the highlight of the birthday. I think the only problem I had was that I did not prepare enough, so my only tip is to make sure that you have plenty because everyone will love it.

Stuffed Focaccia with Spinach, Olives, and Mozzarella

Focaccia Farcita SERVES 6

3½ cups all-purpose white flour

2 teaspoons dried yeast

¼ cup extra virgin olive oil, plus extra for brushing

1 cup warm water

9 ounces frozen spinach, defrosted

7 ounces mozzarella cheese, chopped

¼ cup pitted Kalamata olives, chopped

2 teaspoons fresh thyme leaves, stripped from the sprigs

Coarse sea salt for sprinkling

Salt and freshly ground black pepper

Sift the flour into a large bowl and stir in the yeast. Make a well in the center, pour in the oil, and water and with the help of a wooden spoon, mix all together.

Transfer the mixture on a floured surface and knead for 10 minutes, until the dough is smooth and elastic.

Place the dough into a greased bowl, cover with a clean kitchen towel and leave to rise in a warm place for about 1½ hours, until nearly doubled in size.

Meanwhile, squeeze the defrosted spinach to remove any excess water and place in a large bowl. Add the mozzarella, olives, and thyme. Season with salt and pepper and mix well.

Preheat the oven to 425°F. Brush a 10-inch removable-bottom cake pan with oil.

Knock back the dough by punching it, and divide it into two pieces. Roll out the first piece a little larger than the pan. Place on the bottom of the pan and mold the sides to be higher than the base.

Spread the spinach mixture over the bottom to within ½ in of the edge.

Roll out the remaining dough to the size of the pan, brush the edges with a little water, and place over the filling. Press the edges together to make a good seal.

Using your fingers, press all over the surface and then brush with the extra virgin olive oil. Sprinkle with the salt and bake in the middle of the oven for 30 minutes, until risen and firm.

Remove the focaccia from the oven and allow to rest in the pan for 10 minutes, then place on a wire rack to cool slightly. Enjoy while still warm and fragrant. If you do have any left over, it will still taste great for lunch the next day.

I absolutely love tarts, and it's a shame that not many people cook them anymore, maybe because it is thought to be quite a difficult dish to prepare. Some of my friends have tried this dish and they say that it's definitely one of the easiest and tastiest tart recipes that they have ever made. I often choose this kind of recipe when I have a dinner party because if there is any left over, I'll take it to my office and have it cold for lunch with some salad.

Artichoke and Spinach Tart

Torta di Carciofi e Spinaci SERVES 8

3 tablespoons olive oil

2 onions, thinly sliced

8 artichokes hearts in oil from a jar, drained and halved

14 ounces prepared shortcrust pastry

Flour for dusting

14 ounces baby spinach leaves, roughly chopped

6 eggs

⅛ cup freshly grated Parmesan cheese

3 ounces feta cheese, crumbled

Salt and freshly ground black pepper

Preheat the oven to 350°F.

Heat the olive oil in a large frying pan over medium heat and cook the onions for 5 to 6 minutes, until softened, stirring occasionally. Add the artichokes with 6 tablespoons water, cover the pan, and braise over a gentle heat for 6 minutes.

Roll out the pastry on a lightly floured surface and use to line a 10-inch removable-bottom tart pan. Chill in the freezer for 10 minutes.

Line the tart pan with parchment paper and baking beans, place on a baking sheet, and bake in the middle of the oven for 15 minutes. Remove the paper and beans and set aside to cool.

Meanwhile, blanch the spinach by putting it in a colander over the sink and pouring boiling water over it. Squeeze out the excess water and set aside.

Lightly beat the eggs in a large bowl, and add the cheeses and spinach. Season with salt and pepper and mix well, then stir in the artichokes and onions.

Pour the mixture into the pastry and spread out evenly. Place in the middle of the oven and bake for about 30 minutes, or until the filling is just set.

Allow the tart to cool in the pan for 15 minutes, then remove and transfer to a large plate.

Cut into slices and serve warm with your favorite salad.

This is the ultimate Neapolitan recipe. I still remember my teenage years when I rode around on my scooter with my friends and stopped off in a pizzeria for a quick calzone. I've given a meat and a vegetarian filling here but, of course, you can stuff them with almost anything you want—for example, you can substitute cooked bacon or prosciutto for the cooked ham. Don't prepare this recipe in advance because the filling will make the dough soggy.

Calzone

MAKES 6

FOR THE DOUGH

2 pinches of salt

2 teaspoons dried yeast

1 cup warm water

2¾ cups bread flour, plus extra for dusting

2 tablespoons extra virgin olive oil, plus extra for greasing

FOR THE VEGETARIAN FILLING

18 ounces ricotta cheese

¾ cup freshly grated Pecorino cheese

3½ ounces arugula leaves, chopped

3 ounces pistachios, crushed

Pinch of freshly grated nutmeg

¼ cup extra virgin olive oil

FOR THE MEAT FILLING

½ cup pesto

6 slices cooked ham

6 slices mozzarella

Salt and freshly ground black pepper

To prepare the dough, mix together the salt, yeast, and water in a pitcher. Sift the flour into a large bowl, make a well in the center, and add the yeast mixture along with the olive oil. Use a wooden spoon to mix everything together to create a wet dough.

Turn out the dough onto a clean well-floured surface and work it with your hands for about 5 minutes or until smooth and elastic. Shape into six balls, place on a baking sheet, and cover with a kitchen towel. Leave in a warm place to rest for at least 30 minutes, or until the dough nearly doubles in size.

Preheat the oven to 425°F.

Once rested, turn out the dough balls onto a floured surface. Use your hands (or a rolling pin) to push out from the center to create six round discs, about 6 inches in diameter. Place the pizza bases on oiled baking sheets.

To prepare the vegetarian filling, mix all the ingredients in a large bowl, season with salt and pepper, and divide equally among three pizza bases, placing the filling on one half of each disc.

To prepare the meat filling, spread the pesto equally on the other three bases and top with a slice of ham, two slices of mozzarella, a pinch of salt and pepper, then cover with the remaining ham. Again, make sure you place the filling on one half of each disc.

Gently fold the pizza discs over the filling, creating a half-moon shape, and seal the edges carefully.

Bake in the middle of the oven for about 20 minutes, or until golden brown. Rest the calzone on a wire rack for about a minute, then enjoy with a cold beer.

Rome is known for three important things: the Vatican, the Colosseum, and this fantastic recipe. Usually gnocchi is made with flour and potato, but the Romans like to use semolina. I know that not many people like semolina or polenta but, believe you me, this will surprise you because the flavors are amazing. A great dish to prepare in the morning, ready to be cooked just before your guests arrive. You can use Parmesan instead of Pecorino.

Roman-style Semolina Gnocchi with Tomato and Basil Sauce

Gnocchi alla Romana SERVES 6

2½ cups whole-fat milk

¼ nutmeg, freshly grated

1¼ cup plus 1 tablespoon coarse semolina

10½ tablespoons salted butter

1¾ cup freshly grated Pecorino Romano

4 eggs, beaten

FOR THE SAUCE

6 tablespoons olive oil

1 large onion, thinly sliced

3 x 14-ounce cans chopped tomatoes

15 basil leaves

Salt and freshly ground black pepper

Preheat the oven to 400°F.

Put 2½ cups water, the milk, and nutmeg in a large saucepan and bring to a boil. Sprinkle the semolina into the pan using one hand while whisking constantly with the other hand to prevent lumps from forming. Whisk until the mixture begins to thicken. Change the whisk for a wooden spoon and cook over medium heat for about 10 minutes, stirring constantly. The mixture is ready when it starts to come away from the sides of the pan.

Remove from the heat and mix in a third of the butter, half the cheese, and the eggs. Season with salt and pepper.

Lightly dampen your work surface with cold water and, using a metal spatula, spread the semolina until it is about ¾-inch thick. Allow to cool and firm up.

Once the semolina is firm, use a 2-inch diameter pastry cutter to cut the semolina into even-sized circles.

Use some of the remaining butter to grease a shallow ovenproof serving dish. Arrange a layer of scraps from the leftover semolina on the base of the dish. Lay the semolina circles on top, overlapping.

Sprinkle the remaining cheese on top and dot with little knobs of the remaining butter. Grind over some black pepper and bake in the middle of the oven for about 25 minutes, until golden and bubbling.

Meanwhile, make the sauce. Heat the olive oil in a large saucepan over medium heat and gently cook the onion until softened. Add the chopped tomatoes and basil and season with salt and pepper.

Allow to simmer for 20 minutes, uncovered, stirring occasionally.

Once the gnocchi are cooked, pour some of the sauce in the middle of a serving dish and scoop over the gnocchi. Serve immediately.

In my family, everybody loves chorizo, especially when fried with beans and arugula leaves. So one day I went to buy some fresh squid and came up with this beautiful salad, which is now one of our favorites whenever we have people to dinner. The sweetness of the squid with the spiciness of the chorizo is a perfect match. My only tip is to make sure that you dress the arugula leaves at the last minute, otherwise the leaves will discolor and get soggy.

Squid and Chorizo Salad with Beans and Arugula Leaves

Insalata di Calamari con Fagioli e Chorizo SERVES 6

3½ ounces canned chickpeas, drained

3½ ounces canned borlotti beans, drained

15 cherry tomatoes, quartered

1 medium-hot red chile, seeded and thinly sliced

1 garlic clove, finely chopped

3 tablespoons chopped fresh flat-leaf parsley

2 tablespoons freshly squeezed lemon juice

8 tablespoons extra virgin olive oil

14 ounces medium squid

3 ounces hot chorizo sausage, cut into thin rounds

2 ounces arugula leaves

Salt to taste

Place the chickpeas and beans in a large bowl with the tomatoes, chile, garlic, and parsley. Add the lemon juice with 5 tablespoons of the oil, season with salt, and toss together.

To prepare the squid, pull the head and tentacles from the body pouch. (Work over a bowl or the sink to catch any ink.) Cut off and reserve the tentacles. Remove the beak from the head and discard the intestines. Pull out and discard the quill from inside the body pouch and wash the pouch, inside and out. Cut open the body pouch of each squid along one side and score the inside with the tip of a small sharp knife into a fine diamond pattern. Then cut each pouch first in half lengthwise and then across to give you 3-inch pieces.

Heat the remaining oil in a large frying pan over high heat. Add the reserved tentacles and the squid pieces, scored side upward, which means they will curl attractively. Sear for about 30 seconds, then turn over the pieces and continue to sear for an additional 30 seconds, until golden and caramelized. Season with salt, add the chorizo, and cook for an additional minute, still over high heat.

Toss the arugula leaves with the bean salad and transfer to a large serving plate. Top with the squid and chorizo and serve immediately.

The last three summers I have spent my holiday on the island of Sardinia on the Costa Smeralda, where I learned this wonderful recipe. Sardinia is famous for the production of saffron, and I think that it works perfectly with skate. Use this dish to start a great dinner party, and make sure you serve a good bottle of Italian white wine with it.

Skate with Hot Tomato, Saffron, and Caper Dressing

Razza alla Sarda SERVES 4

6½ tablespoons extra virgin olive oil

½ teaspoon dried crushed chiles

5 garlic cloves, thinly sliced

14 ounces canned plum tomatoes

Pinch of saffron strands

½ ounce golden raisins

2 x 9-ounce skate wings, skinned and trimmed

Salt and freshly ground black pepper

TO SERVE

2 tablespoons small capers in brine, drained and rinsed

16 purple basil leaves

Put the oil in a medium saucepan over medium heat. Add the chiles and garlic and, as soon they start to sizzle, add the tomatoes, saffron, and golden raisins. Season with salt.

Cook gently, uncovered, for about 30 minutes, stirring occasionally with a wooden spoon to allow the tomatoes to break down.

Meanwhile, bring about 1 quart of water to a boil in a large shallow pan. Stir in 1 tablespoon of salt.

Place the skate wings in the boiling salted water and gently simmer for 15 minutes.

Use a fish slice to lift the skate wings out of the water and transfer to a cutting board. Cut each wing into 2 pieces using a sharp knife.

To serve, divide half of the sauce among 4 serving plates, top each one with a piece of skate, and spoon the remaining sauce down the center of the skate.

Scatter with the capers, garnish with the purple basil, and serve immediately.

What a great vegetarian dish—full of colors, flavors and, of course, most important, simple to prepare. I often make this dish when I'm not sure if my guests are vegetarian or not, because I know that even a committed meat eater will like it. You can substitute a good cottage cheese for the ricotta and, if you don't like rosemary, you can always use fresh thyme or chives instead.

Stuffed Red Pimentos with Ricotta, Rosemary, and Chile Olive Oil

Diavoletti Ripieni SERVES 8

10 long thin red pimento peppers

2 tablespoons olive oil

1 tablespoon salted capers, rinsed under cold water and drained

9 ounces ricotta cheese

1 tablespoon fresh rosemary leaves, stripped from the stalks, finely chopped

Juice of 1 small lemon

Chile-flavored olive oil, for drizzling

Salt and freshly ground black pepper

Place the peppers on a cutting board and use a sharp medium knife to cut them lengthwise and remove the seeds.

Place the peppers in a large bowl, drizzle with olive oil, and season with salt and pepper. Toss well.

Heat a grill pan until very hot and cook the peppers until lightly charred on both sides.

Meanwhile, finely chop the capers and place in a bowl with the ricotta, rosemary, and lemon juice. Season with a little salt.

While the peppers are still warm, use a teaspoon to spread the ricotta mixture into the cut sides.

Place the stuffed peppers on a large serving dish, drizzle with chile olive oil, and serve warm as a starter or to accompany your favorite fish dish.

I'm not a big fan of coriander, ginger, or dates. One day I was challenged by a friend to come up with a recipe with these three ingredients that I would serve at a dinner party. To be honest with you, I had a nightmarish two days trying to come up with something that I would enjoy. Then I remembered a great Moroccan recipe that I learned when I was working in Marbella. I know that it may sound funny, but I call this an Italian lamb tagine.

Italian Lamb Tagine

Stufato di Agnello alla Marocchina SERVES 8

3 pound boned leg of lamb, cut into 1¼-inch cubes

1 teaspoon ground ginger

½ teaspoon saffron strands

1 teaspoon ground coriander

4 tablespoons extra virgin olive oil

10½ ounces shallots, unpeeled

1 tablespoon all-purpose flour

2 tablespoons tomato paste

5½ ounces pitted Kalamata olives

2 cups chicken stock

3 tablespoons chopped fresh flat-leaf parsley

1 cinnamon stick

3 ounces pitted dates

2 tablespoons honey

Salt and freshly ground black pepper

Place the lamb in a large bowl with the ginger, saffron, and coriander. Drizzle with 1 tablespoon of oil, mix well, cover with plastic wrap and refrigerate for 6 hours or overnight.

Bring a medium saucepan of water to a boil. Cook the shallots for 2 minutes, drain, refresh in cold water, and peel.

When the meat has marinated, preheat the oven to 350°F.

Heat the remaining oil in a heavy-bottom ovenproof casserole. Add the lamb and start to brown the pieces for about 5 minutes.

Stir in the flour with the tomato paste and continue to cook for an additional 2 minutes, stirring continuously. Add the shallots, olives, stock, parsley, and cinnamon stick. Season with salt and pepper, mix, and bring to a boil.

Cover the casserole with a lid and transfer to the oven. Cook for 1½ hours, stirring occasionally, then remove the cinnamon stick and add the dates and honey. Stir to mix and return to the oven for an additional 20 minutes.

Serve hot with a beautiful lemon couscous (see page 83).

SERVES

4

For anyone who loves turkey but is bored with the traditional ways of cooking it, you have just found the recipe that you need. In my house we have saltimbocca at least once a week because it's easy to prepare and, most important, full of flavor. You can definitely try it with chicken breasts and, if you don't like prosciutto, use pancetta. In the event that you don't have Marsala wine, a good brandy can also be used.

Turkey Saltimbocca with Sage and Prosciutto Ham

Saltimbocca di Tacchino SERVES 4

4 medium turkey breasts

4 slices prosciutto, cut in half widthwise

16 small fresh sage leaves

3 tablespoons olive oil

3½ tablespoons salted butter

¾ cup Marsala wine

Salt and freshly ground black pepper

Place the turkey breasts on a cutting board and cover with plastic wrap. Use a meat mallet to pound out each breast until flattened.

Cut the breasts in half widthwise to give you 8 pieces in total. Season with a little salt and pepper and lay a piece of prosciutto on each breast. Top with 2 sage leaves and secure with a cocktail stick.

Heat the oil and half of the butter in a large frying pan over medium heat. Once hot, place the saltimbocca in the pan, ham side down. Cook for 2 minutes, or until browned. Turn over and cook for an additional 3 minutes, until just cooked through.

Once ready, transfer the saltimbocca onto a plate and cover with foil.

Pour the Marsala wine into the hot frying pan and use a wooden spoon to deglaze the pan by scraping up the meaty bits on the bottom. Simmer over high heat for 2 minutes, until the sauce is slightly reduced. Stir in the remaining butter and season with salt and pepper.

Return the saltimbocca and any juices to the pan, turning them in the sauce for 30 seconds. Remove the pan from the heat and remove the cocktail sticks from the saltimbocca.

Serve 2 pieces of saltimbocca per person on warm serving plates and enjoy accompanied with Cheesy Mashed Potatoes (see page 125). Perfect with a glass of cold dry wine.

For anyone who loves burgers, this has to be the ultimate recipe. To me this is the perfect party food because you can prepare and cook the burgers in advance and just heat them up when needed. The relish too can also be prepared in advance, leaving you time to enjoy your guests rather than spending loads of time in the kitchen. I chose lamb because it gives the burgers a great texture but, if you want, you can try ground beef or pork.

Lamb Burgers with Spicy Tomato and Red Pepper Relish

Burgers di Agnello con Salsina Piccante   SERVES 4

FOR THE BURGERS

1 pound ground lamb

½ red pepper, cored, seeded, and finely chopped

½ onion, finely chopped

⅛ teaspoon chili powder

1 tablespoon ketchup

¼ cup chopped fresh flat-leaf parsley

2 tablespoons extra virgin olive oil

Salt

FOR THE RELISH

1 tablespoon olive oil

½ onion, finely chopped

½ red pepper, cored, seeded, and finely chopped

1 ripe plum tomato, seeded, and diced

⅛ teaspoon sugar

⅛ teaspoon chili powder

1 tablespoon red wine vinegar

2 tablespoons chopped fresh flat-leaf parsley

1 ciabatta loaf, cut in half lengthwise

Place the ground meat in a large bowl with the red pepper, onion, chili powder, ketchup, and parsley. Season with salt and mix well until combined. Divide the mixture into four balls and shape each one into 1¼-inch-thick burgers.

To make the relish, heat the oil in a small frying pan. Add the onion, pepper, tomato, sugar, chili powder, and vinegar. Season with salt and cook over medium heat for 3 minutes, until thickened. Stir in the parsley and set aside to cool.

Heat the extra virgin olive oil in a large frying pan over medium heat and cook the burgers for 6 minutes on each side for a medium burger or for 8 minutes on each side for well-done.

Meanwhile, place the ciabatta on a hot grill pan and cook until golden and crisp on both sides.

Cut the griddled ciabatta pieces in half and arrange on warmed serving plates. Place a lamb burger on each one. Spoon the relish over the top and serve with a few salad leaves and a cold beer.

Many people are too frightened to cook pheasant because they believe it is too complicated to prepare. Well, I will prove that this is not the case with this typical Northern Italian recipe that will leave your guests completely astounded with the flavor and presentation. Please make sure that once the pheasant is cooked, you let it rest for a good ten minutes so it becomes tender. You can try this recipe with a large chicken, if you like.

The Ultimate Roast Pheasant with Vegetables

Fagiano al Forno con Vegetali SERVES 6

2 tablespoons fresh rosemary leaves, stripped from the stalks

2 tablespoons fresh thyme leaves, stripped from the sprigs

8 garlic cloves

1 pheasant, cut in half down the breastbone

3 carrots, unpeeled and cut into 1¼-inch chunks

3 zucchini, cut into 1¼-inch chunks

3 potatoes, peeled and cut into 1¼-inch chunks

6 tablespoons extra virgin olive oil

Salt and freshly ground black pepper

Preheat the oven to 400°F.

Finely chop the rosemary, thyme, and garlic with a sharp knife.

Make several cuts in the skin of the pheasant and stuff the herb mixture into the cuts.

Place the prepared vegetables in a roasting pan, drizzle with half of the oil, season with salt and pepper, and mix well.

Lay the pheasant on top of the vegetables, skin side up, drizzle with the remaining oil, and roast in the middle of the oven for 35 minutes. After the first 15 minutes, baste the pheasant with the cooking juices from the bottom of the pan.

To check that the bird is cooked, pierce each half with a skewer; if the juices run clear, it is ready.

Remove the pheasant from the pan, cut each piece into three, and replace on top of the vegetables. Roast for an additional 5 minutes.

Remove from the oven and rest for 10 minutes to allow the meat to relax and become more tender.

To serve, place the vegetables and pheasant on a large serving plate and enjoy with a beautiful bottle of Italian red wine.

When I was in Italy recently I visited the first restaurant that I worked in when I was a kid, which is called Franco. I had a chance to cook with the owner, Salvatore, and we came up with this beautiful fish recipe that since then has been one of my favorites at my dinner parties. You can substitute trout or sea bass for the salmon and please make sure you use good-quality ripe plum tomatoes.

Baked Whole Salmon with Roasted Tomatoes, Potatoes, and Anchovies

Salmone alla Vesuviana SERVES 4

2¼ pounds potatoes, peeled and cut into ½-inch slices

5 large plum tomatoes, quartered lengthwise

2 red peppers, seeded and cut into 8 chunks

2 yellow peppers, seeded and cut into 8 chunks

2½ ounces anchovy fillets in oil, drained

⅔ cup vegetable stock

6 garlic cloves, halved

4 sprigs fresh oregano

4 sprigs fresh rosemary

6 tablespoons extra virgin olive oil, plus extra for drizzling

1 whole salmon, weighing about 3¼ pound, cleaned, head and tail on

Sea salt and freshly ground black pepper

Preheat the oven to 400°F.

Bring the potatoes to a boil in a large saucepan of salted water and cook for 5 minutes. Drain and arrange the slices over the bottom of a roasting pan large enough to accommodate the whole salmon.

Scatter the tomatoes and peppers over the potatoes. Break the anchovy fillets over the vegetables and pour in the stock. Add the garlic, oregano, and rosemary, and season with salt and pepper.

Pour over the oil and roast in the middle of the oven for 30 minutes.

Meanwhile, slash the salmon 5 times down both sides and then slash in the opposite direction on one side to create an attractive criss-cross pattern. Rub well with more extra virgin olive oil, season with salt and pepper, and place the fish on top of the vegetables.

Return the pan to the oven and continue to roast for an additional 35 to 40 minutes, or until the salmon is cooked through.

Once ready, divide the fish among 4 serving plates, accompanied by the roasted vegetables.

Buonissimo with a cold bottle of Italian dry white wine.

If I have to choose one recipe that will guarantee smiling faces in my house this will definitely be the one. My boys love spareribs in any way I cook them, but this is their absolute favorite. I have tried this dish at many garden and indoor parties and it always works a treat. If you want, once marinated, you can easily cook the ribs on a grill, but please make sure that they are sticky and glossy.

Roasted Pork Spareribs with Maple Syrup and Rosemary

Scottadita allo Sciroppo di Acero SERVES 6

24 pork spareribs

2 tablespoon olive oil

5 tablespoons maple syrup

1 tablespoon chopped fresh rosemary leaves, stripped from the stalks

2 tablespoons soy sauce

1¾ cups apple juice

8 garlic cloves, unpeeled

Salt and freshly ground black pepper

Place the ribs in a large bowl, season with salt and pepper, and add all the other ingredients.

Use your hands to massage the marinade into the ribs. Cover with plastic wrap and leave to rest in the fridge for 15 hours. If you can, massage the ribs with the marinade every 3 hours or so.

Once ready, remove the bowl from the fridge. Preheat the oven to 400°F.

Place the marinated ribs in a large roasting pan, cover with aluminum foil, and cook in the middle of the oven for 15 minutes.

Remove the foil and continue to cook for an additional 30 minutes.

Turn the ribs in the pan and continue to cook for an additional 45 minutes, until the ribs look sticky and glossy.

Place on a large serving platter and serve immediately.

This is a gorgeous dessert that needs very little effort to prepare yet tastes wonderful and looks amazing. I don't think I've ever met anyone yet who doesn't like Amaretti cookies or Amaretto liqueur, so I can guarantee you that everyone will enjoy this unique Italian half-frozen dessert. Make sure you serve it as soon as it's sliced and placed on a serving plate—before it melts too much.

Ice Cream Cake with Nougat and Amaretto

Semifreddo all'Amaretto SERVES 8

Oil for greasing

1 vanilla pod

4 large eggs, separated into 2 large clean dry bowls

¼ cup superfine sugar

2¼ cups heavy cream

12 ounces torrone (almond nougat)

3 tablespoons honey

10 hard Amaretti cookies, crushed (use your hands)

5 tablespoons Amaretto liqueur

Confectioners' sugar, for dusting

Oil a 5-cup, 3-inch-deep mold or loaf pan and line it with two layers of plastic wrap.

Slit the vanilla pod lengthwise, scrape out the seeds, and place in the bowl with the egg yolks. (Don't waste the vanilla pod: place it in a jar of sugar to create beautiful vanilla-flavored sugar.) Beat in the sugar for about 5 minutes using an electric mixer until the mixture is thick and pale.

Clean the beaters and beat the cream into soft peaks.

Clean the beaters again and beat the egg whites into stiff peaks.

Place the torrone in a plastic bag and smash it into small pieces using a rolling pin.

Gently fold the whipped cream, honey, cookies, and nougat into the egg yolk mixture. Fold in the egg whites with the Amaretto liqueur and spoon the mixture into the prepared mold or loaf pan.

Cover the top of the mixture with plastic wrap and place in the freezer to rest for at least 5 hours.

To serve, remove from the freezer and allow it to thaw slightly (about 3 to 5 minutes). Remove the plastic wrap, turn out the cake, and cut into ¾-inch thick slices.

Place 2 slices on a serving plate, dust with a little confectioners' sugar, and serve with your favorite cup of coffee.

If you are a trifle lover and fancy something with a bit more of a kick, this is the recipe to try. Of course I had to put a bit of an Italian twist in, so I used Limoncello liqueur and mascarpone cheese. If you can't find Pandoro or Panettone, you can use a good-quality sponge cake instead and make sure you use a glass serving dish so you can see the colorful layers in the trifle.

Limoncello Trifle

Zuppa Inglese al Limoncello SERVES 8

2 cups superfine sugar

7 tablespoons Limoncello liqueur

10½ ounces blueberries

½ teaspoon arrowroot, mixed to a smooth paste with 2 tablespoons cold water

5 eggs, separated

9 ounces mascarpone cheese

6 heaping tablespoons lemon curd

1 Pandoro cake, cut into ¾-inch slices (or Panettone)

2⅓ cups heavy cream

Handful of toasted slivered almonds

Put half the sugar and ½ cup water in a medium saucepan and dissolve over medium heat. Cook for 5 minutes, stirring occasionally.

Measure off 6 tablespoons of the sugar syrup into a bowl, pour in the Limoncello, mix well, and set aside to cool.

Add most of the blueberries to the pan with the remaining sugar syrup and cook over medium heat for 2 minutes, until they are beginning to release some of their juice. (Reserve a few for decoration.)

Stir the arrowroot paste into the pan with the blueberries and cook for an additional minute, stirring continuously. Allow to cool.

Place the egg yolks and the remaining sugar in a large bowl and beat until pale and thick. Beat in the mascarpone cheese and lemon curd.

In a separate clean dry bowl, beat the egg whites until soft peaks form. Gently fold into the mascarpone cheese and lemon curd mixture.

Place a layer of Pandoro in a large 5-cup glass serving bowl. Brush with a third of the Limoncello syrup, then spread with a third of the curd mixture. Top with a third of the berries and their syrup. Repeat the layers twice, brushing the cake with the remaining Limoncello syrup, and making sure the top layer is the lemon curd mixture.

Cover the bowl with plastic wrap and chill for 5 hours or overnight.

To serve, beat the cream to soft peaks and spread evenly over the trifle. Scatter with the reserved blueberries and toasted slivered almonds.

This is what I call a wow dessert. Don't be afraid of making the pavlova because if you try it my way it will always work. It's a fantastic dessert that can be served at a summer or winter party—the only difference would be to change the type of berries that you use. For maximum satisfaction, use fresh basil and not the dried stuff that comes in jars.

Strawberry Pavlova with Basil, Lime, and Balsamic Vinegar

Pavlova con Fragole e Aceto Balsamico SERVES 8

6 large egg whites

1⅛ cups superfine sugar (preferably from a jar in which you have buried a couple of vanilla pods)

1 teaspoon white wine vinegar

2 teaspoons cornstarch

2 tablespoons finely chopped fresh basil

Zest of 1 lime and 1 teaspoon lime juice

FOR THE TOPPING

14 ounces fresh strawberries, cut in half

3 tablespoons superfine sugar (see left)

2 tablespoons finely chopped fresh basil plus 8 small basil leaves to decorate

2 teaspoons balsamic vinegar

2 cups heavy cream

Few drops of vanilla extract

Line a baking sheet with parchment paper and draw a 10-inch diameter circle on it. Preheat the oven to 350°F.

Put the egg whites in a large clean dry bowl and beat until stiff. The whisk should make a stiff peak when drawn out of the egg whites.

Beat in half of the sugar and continue to beat until the mixture is thick and glossy. Use a spatula to fold in the remaining sugar, then the vinegar, cornstarch, basil, and lime zest and juice.

Spoon the meringue onto the baking sheet, following the circle. Make a dip in the center with the back of a spoon and create peaks at the edges.

Place in the middle of the oven and bake for 5 minutes. Reduce the temperature to 275°F and continue to bake for an additional hour. Turn off the heat and leave the meringue in the oven for at least 5 hours or overnight.

Once the meringue is ready, place the strawberries in a bowl and toss with the sugar, chopped basil, and balsamic vinegar. Leave to marinate for 1 hour, tossing occasionally.

About 30 minutes before serving, beat the cream in a large bowl with the vanilla extract until soft peaks form. Pile the cream onto the meringue base.

Arrange the strawberries on top, using a slotted spoon.

Just before serving, spoon over the juices and decorate with the small basil leaves.

SERVES
8

What a wonderful way to end a meal. Very impressive, very tasty, very colorful, and very, very healthy. OK, maybe not that healthy, but come on, once in a while it has to be done. To make your life easier, you can prepare the raspberry sauce a couple of hours in advance and if you want, once the soufflés are ready, make a hole in the center and pour in the sauce. This is a dessert to remember!

Hot Chocolate Soufflés with Raspberry and Grand Marnier Sauce

Soufflés al Cioccolato con Salsa di Lamponi SERVES 6

2 tablespoons salted butter, at room temperature, for greasing

10½ ounces dark chocolate (at least 70 percent cocoa solids)

4 egg yolks

8 egg whites

½ cup superfine sugar, plus extra for sprinkling

Confectioners' sugar for dusting

FOR THE SAUCE

½ pound raspberries

½ cup confectioners' sugar

¼ cup red wine

¼ cup Grand Marnier

Preheat the oven to 425°F. Butter six individual ramekin dishes, sprinkle with a little superfine sugar, and shake out any excess. Chill until ready to use.

Melt the chocolate in a heatproof bowl over a pan of simmering water. Make sure that the water doesn't touch the base of the bowl. Once the chocolate has melted, leave to cool slightly. Gently beat in the 4 egg yolks, one at a time, until the mixture thickens.

Beat the egg whites in a large clean dry bowl until stiff. Whisk in the superfine sugar, a tablespoon at a time.

Fold a little of the egg white mixture into the melted chocolate, then fold the chocolate mix into the remaining beaten egg whites until evenly combined.

Divide the soufflé mixture among the prepared ramekins. Run your finger between the inside edge of each ramekin and the mixture to make a small groove to help the soufflés rise evenly.

Place the ramekins on a baking sheet and bake in the middle of the oven for 12 to 14 minutes, until well risen and just wobbly in the middle.

Meanwhile, make the sauce. Puree the raspberries in a food processor, then puree through a sieve into a small saucepan.

Add the confectioners' sugar, wine, and Grand Marnier. Bring to a simmer and cook for 5 minutes, until slightly reduced, stirring occasionally.

Dust the soufflés with confectioners' sugar and serve immediately with the warm sauce.

My late grandfather nonno Giovanni was renowned for this dessert. It was created by him about 35 years ago, when he used to have a restaurant on the island of Sardinia. Although I wasn't even born when this dish was created, I feel as if there is a special bond between us, as I would have picked exactly the same ingredients and cooked it exactly the same way. You can substitute Limoncello liqueur for the Grand Marnier.

Orange and Grand Marnier Upside-Down Cake

Torta alle Arance e Grand Marnier SERVES 8

¾ cup granulated sugar

4 oranges, peeled and sliced into ¼-inch slices

3 large eggs

½ cup superfine sugar

1 teaspoon baking powder

2 tablespoons grated orange zest

1 cup all-purpose flour, sifted

3 tablespoons Grand Marnier, to serve

Preheat the oven to 350°F.

Make the caramel by combining the granulated sugar with 3 teaspoons water in a small nonstick pan. Place over medium heat, stirring occasionally until dissolved. Once the sugar mixture is gently boiling and starting to darken, remove the pan from the heat and pour the caramel into the base of an 8-inch flan dish.

Gently push the orange slices into the caramel, arranged slightly overlapping. Set aside.

Put the eggs in a large bowl and beat until fluffy and nearly double in size. Add the superfine sugar and continue to beat until creamy and thick.

Add the baking powder and orange zest and continue to beat until the mixture forms thick ribbons. Gradually add the flour and fold it in carefully to retain as much air in the mixture as possible.

Pour the mixture into the flan dish over the orange slices and bake in the middle of the oven for 25 minutes. To test the cake is done insert a toothpick in the center of the sponge and if it comes out clean the sponge is ready.

Remove the dish from the oven and use a knife to cut around the edge of the sponge.

Wearing oven mitts, place a serving plate over the top of the flan dish and quickly invert the plate and the dish to turn out the orange sponge. (Be careful, as the caramel sauce will be very hot.)

Drizzle over the Grand Marnier and serve at room temperature with a good-quality vanilla ice cream.

Conversion chart

Weight (solids)

7g	¼oz
10g	½oz
20g	¾oz
25g	1oz
40g	1½oz
50g	2oz
60g	2½oz
75g	3oz
100g	3½oz
110g	4oz (¼lb)
125g	4½oz
150g	5½oz
175g	6oz
200g	7oz
225g	8oz (½lb)
250g	9oz
275g	10oz
300g	10½oz
310g	11oz
325g	11½oz
350g	12oz (¾lb)
375g	13oz
400g	14oz
425g	15oz
450g	1lb
500g (½kg)	18oz
600g	1¼lb
700g	1½lb
750g	1lb 10oz
900g	2lb
1kg	2¼lb
1.1kg	2½lb
1.2kg	2lb 12oz
1.3kg	3lb
1.5kg	3lb 5oz
1.6kg	3½lb
1.8kg	4lb
2kg	4lb 8oz
2.25kg	5lb
2.5kg	5lb 8oz
3kg	6lb 8oz

Volume (liquids)

5ml	1 teaspoon
10ml	1 dessertspoon
15ml	1 tablespoon or ½fl oz
30ml	1fl oz
40ml	1½fl oz
50ml	2fl oz
60ml	2½fl oz
75ml	3fl oz
100ml	3½fl oz
125ml	4fl oz
150ml	5fl oz (¼ pint)
160ml	5½fl oz
175ml	6fl oz
200ml	7fl oz
225ml	8fl oz
250ml (0.25 liter)	9fl oz
300ml	10fl oz (½ pint)
325ml	11fl oz
350ml	12fl oz
370ml	13fl oz
400ml	14fl oz
425ml	15fl oz (¾ pint)
450ml	16fl oz
500ml (0.5 liter)	18fl oz
550ml	19fl oz
600ml	20fl oz (1 pint)
700ml	1¼ pints
850ml	1½ pints
1 liter	1¾ pints
1.2 liters	2 pints
1.5 liters	2½ pints
1.8 liters	3 pints
2 liters	3½ pints

Length

5mm	¼ inch
1cm	½ inch
2cm	¾ inch
2.5cm	1 inch
3cm	1¼ inches
4cm	1½ inches
5cm	2 inches
7.5 cm	3 inches
10cm	4 inches
15cm	6 inches
18cm	7 inches
20cm	8 inches
24cm	10 inches
28cm	11 inches
30 cm	12 inches

Oven temperatures

Celsius*	Farenheit	Gas	Description
110°C	225°F	Gas Mark ¼	cool
120°C	250°F	Gas Mark ½	cool
130°C	275°F	Gas Mark 1	very low
150°C	300°F	Gas Mark 2	very low
160°C	325°F	Gas Mark 3	low
180°C	350°F	Gas Mark 4	moderate
190°C	375°F	Gas Mark 5	mod. hot
200°C	400°F	Gas Mark 6	hot
220°C	425°F	Gas Mark 7	hot
230°C	450°F	Gas Mark 8	very hot
240°C	475°F	Gas Mark 9	very hot

* For fan-assisted ovens, reduce temperatures by 10°C

Temperature conversion

$C = 5/9 (F-32)$

$F = 9/5 C + 32$

Index

Almonds
  creamy rice pudding with
    Amaretto and toasted
    almonds, 71
Artichoke and spinach tart, 145
Arugula
  baked omelette with sun-
    dried tomatoes, arugula, and
    feta cheese, 111
  bruschette with roasted pepper
    and cannelloni puree, black
    olive relish, and arugula, 79
  arugula and lemon couscous,
    83
  sliced steak with cherry
    tomatoes, arugula, and
    balsamic vinegar dressing,
    60
  squid and chorizo salad with
    beans and arugula leaves,
    148
Asparagus
  asparagus and ricotta tarts, 24
  spring chilled asparagus soup,
    53

Bananas
  banana fritters with quick
    caramel sauce, 39
  strawberry, banana, and
    tarragon smoothie, 71
Borlotti beans
  Italian bean curry, 56
  squid and chorizo salad with
    beans and arugula leaves,
    148
Beef
  beef tenderloin with flamed
    brandy and green
    peppercorns, 36
  Neapolitan spicy meatballs in
    tomato sauce, 131
  No. 1 lasagna, 99
  rigatoni with white ragu, 97
  sliced steak with cherry
    tomatoes, arugula, and
    balsamic vinegar dressing, 60

Beet rosti with smoked salmon
  and horseradish cream, 115
Bread
  calzone, 146
  chocolate and rum bread and
    butter pudding, 100
  crispy breadsticks with
    Pecorino cheese and thyme,
    142
  stuffed focaccia with spinach,
    olives, and mozzarella, 143

Bruschette with roasted pepper
  and cannellini puree, black
  olive relish, and arugula, 79
Brussels sprouts with garlic
  breadcrumbs and Pecorino,
  63

Calf liver with black pepper,
  butter, and sage, 54
Calzone, 146
Campari served with Parmesan
  crisps, 142
Cannellini beans
  bruschette with roasted pepper
    and cannellini puree, black
    olive relish, and arugula, 79
  chunky winter vegetable and
    bean soup 80
  Italian bean curry, 56
Carrots
  honey-glazed carrots with
    macadamia nuts, 26
  Italian vegetable bake, 98
  spicy carrot soup with garlic
    croutons, 16
Cauliflower curry 89
Cheese
  asparagus and ricotta tarts, 24
  baked omelette with sun-dried
    tomatoes, arugula, and feta
    cheese, 111
  Brussels sprouts with garlic
    breadcrumbs and Pecorino,
    63
  Campari served with Parmesan

crisps, 142
  cheesy mashed potatoes with
    chives, 125
  crispy breadsticks with
    Pecorino cheese and thyme,
    142
  herbed potato pancakes with
    bubbling goat cheese, 51
  onion soup with cheesy
    croutons, 90
  pasta with mushrooms, peas,
    and mascarpone, 126
  pasta with smoked pancetta,
    eggs, and Pecorino Romano,
    34
  playboy eggs, 47
  quick ham and Emmental salad
    with Dijon mustard dressing,
    123
  roasted eggplant with red
    onions and goat cheese, 86
  spicy gammon steak with
    mascarpone peas, 69
  stuffed focaccia with spinach,
    olives, and mozzarella, 143
  stuffed red pimentos with
    ricotta, rosemary, and chile
    olive oil, 152
  stuffed roasted tomatoes with
    goat cheese and mozzarella,
    122
  ultimate macaroni cheese, 93
Chickpeas, hot and spicy, 89
Chicken
  chicken breast in Martini sauce,
    35
  chicken wrapped in prosciutto
    ham with a creamy herb
    sauce, 66
Chicken livers
  garlic chicken liver paté with
    green peppercorns, 68
  honey chicken liver salad with
    sherry vinegar, 26
Chocolate
  chocolate and pistachio crunch
    bars, 135

chocolate and rum bread and
    butter pudding, 100
  chocolate tiramisu, 134
  hot chocolate fondants stuffed
    with chocolate truffles, 41
  hot chocolate soufflés with
    raspberry and Grand
    Marnier sauce, 169
  vanilla ice cream with hot
    espresso, Amaretto, and
    grated chocolate, 40
  white chocolate mousse with
    black pepper and fresh mint,
    136
Chorizo
  squid and chorizo salad with
    beans and arugula leaves,
    148
Clams
  pasta with clams, rosemary, and
    porcini mushrooms, 91
  quick stew of mussels and
    clams, 20
  razor clams with olive oil, lime,
    and chile flakes, 57
Zucchini and lemon zest pasta, 64
Couscous, arugula and lemon, 83
Curry
  cauliflower curry 89
  Italian bean curry, 56

Eggplant, roasted with red onions
    and goat cheese, 86

Eggs
  baked omelette with sun-dried
    tomatoes, arugula, and feta
    cheese, 111
  pasta with smoked pancetta,
    eggs, and Pecorino Romano,
    34
  playboy eggs, 47

Fava beans
  Pecorino and fava bean
    salad with capers, 119

Gammon, spicy steak with
    mascarpone peas, 69
Gnocchi
    little gnocchi with truffle oil,
        butter, and sage, 15
    Roman-style semolina gnocchi
        with tomato and basil sauce,
        147
Green bean salad with mint, goat
    cheese, and pine nuts, 48

Ham. *See also* Prosciutto
    quick ham and Emmental salad
        with Dijon mustard
        dressing, 123

Ice cream
    ice cream cake with nougat and
        Amaretto, 162
    vanilla ice cream with hot
        espresso, Amaretto, and
        grated chocolate, 40
Italian bean curry, 56
Italian lamb tagine, 153
Italian shrimp cocktail, 52
Italian toad in the hole with
    rosemary and red onions, 92
Italian vegetable bake, 98

Lamb
    Italian lamb tagine, 153
    lamb burgers with spicy tomato
        and red pepper relish, 156
    lamb cutlets Tina-style, 67
    rigatoni with white ragu, 97
    roasted lamb shank in red wine
        sauce with Italian mashed
        potatoes, 94
    slow-roasted shoulder of lamb
        with lemon potatoes, 128
Leeks
    roasted monkfish with baby
        leeks and cherry tomatoes,
        27
    salmon and creamy leek
        pastries, 23
Lemon
    arugula and lemon couscous, 83
    best lemon and mango tart,
        103
    fresh salmon and lemon
        mousse, 82
    veal with butter, sage, and
        lemon sauce, 130

zucchini and lemon zest pasta,
    64
Lentils
    Italian bean curry, 56
    lentils and nuts with chive and
        sherry vinegar dressing, 122
Limoncello
    Limoncello and lime granita,
        133
    Limoncello trifle, 165

Mango
    best lemon and mango tart,
        103
Meringues
    marzipan-stuffed peach with
        meringue, 72
    strawberry pavlova with basil,
        lime, and balsamic vinegar,
        166
Monkfish, roasted with baby leeks
    and cherry tomatoes, 27
Mushrooms
    pasta with clams, rosemary, and
        porcini mushrooms,
        91
    pasta with mushrooms, peas,
        and mascarpone, 126
    playboy eggs, 47
Mussels
    quick stew of mussels and
        clams, 20

Neapolitan spicy meatballs in
    tomato sauce, 131

Onions
    Italian toad in the whole with
        rosemary and red onions, 92
    onion soup with cheesy
        croutons, 90
    roasted eggplant with red
        onions and goat cheese,
        86
    roasted onions in rosemary and
        balsamic vinegar, 86
Orange and Grand Marnier
    upside-down cake, 170
Oysters in sesame seeds and black
    peppers tempura, 19

Pancetta
    creamy scallops with pancetta,
        29

pasta with smoked pancetta,
    eggs, and Pecorino Romano,
    34
playboy eggs, 47
rigatoni with white ragu, 97
warm potato and crispy bacon
    salad, 51
Pasta
    zucchini and lemon zest pasta,
        64
    No. 1 lasagna, 99
    pasta with clams, rosemary,
        and porcini mushrooms, 91
    pasta with mushrooms, peas,
        and mascarpone, 126
    pasta with smoked pancetta,
        eggs, and Pecorino Romano,
        34
    pasta with walnut and caper
        pesto, 116
    rigatoni with white ragu, 97
    stuffed pasta shells, 33
    ultimate macaroni cheese, 93
Paté
    garlic chicken liver paté with
        green peppercorns, 68
Peach
    marzipan-stuffed with
        meringue, 72
Peas
    fresh pea and parsley soup, 112
    pasta with mushrooms, peas,
        and mascarpone, 126
    spicy gammon steak with
        mascarpone peas, 69
Peppers
    bruschette with roast pepper
        and cannellini puree, black
        olive relish, and arugula, 79
    lamb burgers with spicy
        tomato and red pepper
        relish, 156
    stuffed red pimentos with
        ricotta, rosemary, and chili
        olive oil, 152
Pheasant, roast with vegetables,
    158
Pizza Vesuvio, 127
Pork
    rigatoni with white ragu, 97
    roasted pork spare ribs with
        maple syrup and rosemary,
        161
Potatoes

baked whole salmon with
    roasted tomatoes, potatoes,
    and anchovies, 160
beet rosti with smoked salmon
    and horseradish cream, 115
cheesy mashed potatoes with
    chives, 125
herby potato cakes with
    bubbling goat cheese, 51
roasted lamb shank in red wine
    sauce with Italian mashed
    potatoes, 94
slow-roasted shoulder of lamb
    with lemon potatoes, 128
warm potato and crispy bacon
    salad, 51
Prosciutto ham
    chicken wrapped in prosciutto
        ham with a creamy herb
        sauce, 66
    risotto with prosciutto ham and
        Vin Santo, 85
    turkey saltimbocca with sage
        and prosciutto ham, 155

Raspberries
    hot chocolate soufflés with
        raspberry and Grand
        Marnier sauce, 169
    strawberries and raspberries
        layered with whiskey cream,
        104
Rice
    creamy rice pudding with
        Amaretto and toasted
        almonds, 71
    risotto with prosciutto ham and
        Vin Santo, 85

Salad
    French bean salad with mint,
        goat cheese, and pine nuts,
        48
    fresh and tasty tomato salad, 16
    honey chicken liver salad with
        sherry vinegar, 26
    Pecorino and fava bean salad
        with capers, 119
    quick ham and Emmental salad
        with Dijon mustard dressing,
        123
    squid and chorizo salad with
        beans and arugula leaves,
        148